What Every
SUCCESSFUL
❧ PERSON ❧
KNOWS

CARL CASANOVA

WHAT EVERY
SUCCESSFUL
❦ PERSON ❦
KNOWS

6 SELF-COACH SUCCESS STRATEGIES TO MOTIVATE YOUR LIFE

Advantage™

Published by Advantage, Charleston, South Carolina.
Member of Advantage Media Group.

ADVANTAGE is a registered trademark and the Advantage colophon is a trademark of Advantage Media Group, Inc.

Printed in the United States of America.

ISBN: 978-1-59932-052-6
LCCN: 2007937132

Most Advantage Media Group titles are available at special quantity discounts for bulk purchases for sales promotions, premiums, fundraising, and educational use. Special versions or book excerpts can also be created to fit specific needs.

For more information, please write: Special Markets, Advantage Media Group, P.O. Box 272, Charleston, SC 29402 or call 1.866.775.1696.

In memory of my wise and loving grandfather who was my very first success (life) coach

Santiago Velez

(1898-1996)

Table of Contents

Introduction

I ATTENDED A SEMINAR some years ago when the speaker said, "Some people succeed because they are destined to, but most people succeed because they are determined to." When I heard that statement a jolt illuminated within me. It was specifically the last two words, "determined to," that aroused my soul. It was like a declaration of truth for my personal quest for success. Mark me in bold letters under the category of "most people succeed because they are determined to." I am determined to succeed. You may be under that category, as well, a traveler on the road of life with a determination to succeed and help others do the same.

Achievement and success are big topics in our society and our personal lives today. Well, what brings success? Why does success seem to come a little easier for some than for others? Is it possibly due to early opportunities, a supportive family, recognition or high intelligence? Whatever the case, we are all unique, special, and different, and we've all landed on various routes on life's pathways. One thing is certain: each of us is on an expedition, whether we are conscious of it or not and we all want it to lead to a healthy and successful life. One important life lesson I've learned and that is success is fulfilling, renewing and sweet to the soul. Can you remember your initial attempt at being successful at something, anything? Can you recall the seeds of achievement that were planted early? I remember the seeds of success that were planted, nurtured, and evolved early in my developmental years and how they have grown to be a harvest of inspriation and a source of focus day after day, month after month, and year after year.

Most adults can vividly recall their junior high school years (ages 12-15). Psychologists and educators confirm that those middle school years are important transitional and often difficult times for a young person. I remember my challenges from that period of time and how they left an impression that has been a positive source of motivation in my determination to succeed.

At seven years old, my family and I moved to Grand Rapids, Michigan from New York City, which was an absolute culture shock for me. We had moved away from my loving Puerto Rican grandparents, my cousins and other family and friends, whom I missed dearly. Some years later, when I was going into junior high, we moved into a new school district, and I again adjusted to new surroundings and new friends. I enjoyed school and I found a real source of exhilaration in playing sports. Entering into junior high I set a goal for myself: to try out for the first squad on the Seventh grade basketball team. I dedicated my time and I worked hard to excel. I practiced on the fundamentals to improve my shot, my dribble, my defense, and to be a positive contributor on a winning team. This was my first attempt to be a success.

After a week, the tryouts were over, and with my hopes high on making the first playing squad, I went to check the list of those players who made the team that was posted on the boy's locker room bulletin board. I searched intensely for my name to see if I would play on the first squad. I looked again closely. I didn't see my name on the first squad or the second. I didn't make the Seventh grade basketball team. It felt like my entire existence was crushed. I put so much hope into something I wanted and I didn't get it. I walked home that winter day deflated.

I moved on and decided to try again the next year. I surely didn't want to quit, I loved playing sports. I went through the school year practicing as much as I could; determined to make the next year's eighth grade basketball team.

The following year had arrived and I was ready for the tryouts. The coach of the Seventh grade team was the same person for the eighth grade team. To this day I still remember him. Tryouts were competitive but I felt confident it was my year and I would make the team. Now was the moment of truth for me. Feeling excited and a bit anxious I walked to the same locker room bulletin board to check the list as I had done the previous year. I got the same results. Again I was cut from the team. It seemed to me at an early age that I was learning more about failure than about success. I felt I was right back in the valley of despair. I walked around feeling low with little eye contact toward others. I kept to myself and I didn't want others to know my sense of inadequacy. My inner language or self-talk was negative, and my self image felt crushed. I would think to myself, "Why is this happening? Why am I no good?" "How come other players made the team and I didn't?" "What's wrong with me?" "Will I ever be good enough?" All this was going through my head just from not making the junior high basketball team.

I never made the seventh or eighth grade basketball team but my experience during those middle school years taught me two life-long valuable lessons that set the course for my adult journey. One, I had tasted failure and I didn't like it. Two, I developed a deep desire to be successful in life. I wanted to learn and grasp this wonderful thing called "success" and to be successful in all areas of my life. Sure, we all have experienced various bumps in the road — it's unavoidable, and we're human, but it's just that some people don't get past those early setbacks.

My colleague and friend, Dave Krueger, M.D. , author of 16 books including the best selling book, *The Secret Language of Money*, stated, "ninety percent of our lives will be characterized by how we handle the 10% of what happens to us, yet most people look at that 10% and think of it as the 90% that characterizes their lives." In other words, it is not so much what happens to you, it 's what you do with what happens. It is never too late to turn your setbacks into successes.

Not making the team helped define me. I realized that life is not easy and requires much effort. Scott Peck in his classic book *The Road Less Traveled* states it pragmatically in his first chapter saying, "Life is difficult. This is a great truth, one of the greatest truths. It is a great truth because once we truly see this truth, we transcend it." That means we rise above it and when we do it's a launching to lift us in the right direction: a direction toward success.

Some say success is a journey, not a destination. I believe it's both. It is a journey with its amazing adventures of living as a human being, and it is a destination because you must have a specific target in view to aim toward or you'll be what Zig Ziglar, the popular motivational statesman, calls a "wandering generality." Success: it is both a journey and a destination.

USING THIS BOOK

We will learn what successful people know so you can apply it to your own journey in your own way and toward your chosen destination.

The success of others leaves clues for us to follow. As part of my study to find out what successful people know, I have read, researched, and spent time with successful business owners, sales people, entrepreneurs, professionals, parents, athletes, couples, clergy, clients, and many others in order to gather and record the knowledge of success that will benefit us all. We must pay attention to the success in our lives, to the success of the lives around us, and the positive success of the world at large.

My goal was to synthesize success as a realistic formula in six different categories, which comprise the six chapters. It was important for me to write this book as a reminder to myself and to the world of how healthy, how necessary, and how powerful true success really is for all of us. You will discover, as I did, that success is all around us.

This book is to be used as a guide to coach yourself and others. No matter what your job, gender, career status, or stage of life, you'll discover ways to enhance your understanding of success and to maximize all your possibilities for the future. We spend the majority of our energy, time, and money figuring out how to be successful. And why not? It's what everyone wants. Follow the "Six A" steps:

1. Assess
2. Apply
3. Access
4. Assemble
5. Act
6. Advance

I know these steps work, because I have used them to shape my destiny of success. They will help you ascend into deep possibilities for your life success. You will be a living testimony to how these concepts will enlighten and direct you toward accomplishment. The steps are a comprehensive outline to expand your philosophy and use for masterful living.

Please allow me to serve you as your personal success coach using the "Six A" steps proven concepts that will maximize your potential. Each chapter is sequential and designed as a fine-tuned building process with the intention to lift you up and accelerate you forward to a more successful way of living your life both personally and professionally. It also includes field activities to apply as well as six very important points (VIP's) from those who know best about success.

Tryouts for success are held daily in our lives- we must show up, play to win, and never give up. A wise mentor in my profession once said to me, "Carl, you begin everything with faith, so trust the process before you." With your commitment to becoming successful you will eventually join a special group of individuals who also have selected this pilgrammage and eventually witnessed their name on the "made-it list." So, come on....get in the game, it's your life were talking about! You must not settle, for the reward is a long, powerful and well lived life.

Norman Vincent Peale, a pioneer of enhancing success thinking, said, "Begin where you are. Begin now." The best time to step toward your purpose to reach your destination is this present moment; that's why it is essential not to delay. An ancient Chinese saying declares, "a journey of a thousand miles begins with a single step." Believe this, it's a guarantee if you don't take your first step you won't reach your destination." So take your initial step. You have been called to navigate this excursion of your life and the journey has just begun. Welcome! Reading this book is the first indicator that you are ready. This voyage will transform your soul because you have awakened yourself to the potential of your own life. The world is watching. The world is waiting. The world will benefit because of your decision to succeed. Here is my contribution. Enjoy!

"The desire to accomplish is sweet to the soul."

— PROVERBS 13:19

Chapter One
Step 1: Assess Success to Ignite Your Best

TO ASSESS SUCCESS YOU MUST BE ABLE TO PERSONALLY
CLARIFY, AND SPECIFICALLY IDENTIFY THIS CONCEPT CALLED
SUCCESS BEFORE THE LAUNCHING TAKES PLACE.

Successful people know that life is a journey. It begins with astonishing potential and unlimited possibilities. This rite of passage is shaped by many factors, including our beliefs, our environment, our experiences, our vision, our relationships, and our passions. Our travels take us to some wondrous places, but along the way – if we're fully aware during our pilgrimmage – we mature, we evolve, and we realize what's truly significant – health, family, values, goals, and security, are essentials of a fulfilling and happy life. Life experience is directly interwoven into the process of creating and sustaining success during our sojourn on this earth. For people who are committed to be their best the reality is this: to be, and to have, success is the great aim, ambition, and motivation of our lives. This is why we get up each and every morning and why we move onward toward accomplishment and purpose. Observe closely and listen, you will find the subject of success (even subliminally) in almost every interaction. It's universal, it's interconnected, and it's essential.

There is a great desire in our society to not just guess at what success is really like, but to actually experience it at home, at work, in our activities, and our private lives. Abraham Lincoln, who, despite having no formal education became an entrepreneur, a lawyer, and our sixteenth President, once said, "Your own resolution to succeed is more important than any other thing." Success is not only the American dream, it is a universal dream; everyone wants to succeed. The Law of Clarity says that the clearer you are about a specific topic the greater ability you have to acquire what you want. So, let's clarify what we mean by success.

1.1 What is This Thing Called Success?

What an individual thinks or feels as success is unique with him. In our experience we have found that each individual has a different meaning of, and attitude toward, what constitutes success

— ALFRED ADLER

Just talking about success is an inspiring and motivational experience. Observe the response within yourself and the body language of those around you when the subject is discussed. No doubt, success is what everyone wants! Who wants the alternative? "We play to win the game," said a well-known National Football League coach, named Herman Edwards. I have often heard speakers and read books that use the metaphor of life as a game to be played, and when we enter into the game of life it is to win, to succeed at living. I recommend the book *If*

Life is a Game These are the Rules by Cherie Carter Scott, PhD. If you see life as a game, then the objective is to find the strategies to be successful, and the game of life is no exception.

It is absolutely true to say that we all want to personally win and have success. However, the majority of our population is unaware or uninformed as to how to create or sustain the success they really want and desire most. In exploring this subject called "success," one does not have to go too far to obtain a popular and worldly mindset regarding success in our society – the big three: money, fame, and power. In our world today, obtaining these elements often catapult one toward success, or at least it's perceived that way. However, sometime later the person who obtains elite pinnacles faces the question: Could this be all there is? Just being wealthy, or having a high position, or being well known for your accomplishment, is this success?

Sure, these elements, in whatever context you measure them, could, and often do, have a connection; but could there be something missing? From my understanding, there does seem to be much more to the subject of success. There are millions of stories of well-established people who have had money, fame, and power, and if you were to talk to them at a certain point in their lives they would feel they still were not winning or successful in life. They were still waiting for success even though they had what seemed to be everything under the sun. So what is success?

In my search for the definition of success, I've concluded there are no simple or predictable answers. Every human being measures success in their own way; it's left up to the beholder. It means different things to different people. My own philosophy, experience, aspirations, and dreams of success may be completely different from others'. As humans we all come from many cultures and beliefs. We all have distinct meanings, perspective or viewpoints on what success is, and that is okay. We certainly cannot say or control what success should be, could be, or ought to be for someone else. We can see success only through our own eyes and how it makes sense to us individually. How success makes us content, happy, positive, and at peace in our own way is significant and what matters most to us. That is the beauty of success.

Success is a personal and unique journey. The true essence of success, beyond achievements, goals reached, accomplishments, and desires obtained lies solely and completely in our own brain and inner sense of personal and professional fulfillment. Success is totally self-defined. We must evaluate, we must give it meaning, we must give it its distinction from our own life experience. A criterion to define your personal success would be to imagine yourself in a deep sleep and the next morning waking up to the ability to have, to do, or to be anything your heart and soul desires. What would show up? How would you feel? How does this link to your definition of success?

> SUCCESS IS TOTALLY SELF-DEFINED. WE MUST EVALUATE, WE MUST GIVE IT MEANING, WE MUST GIVE IT ITS DISTINCTION FROM OUR OWN LIFE EXPERIENCE.

Identifying success comes down to your own individual interpretation and what it will take for you to feel connected and accomplished in whatever undertaking you advance toward. As a success-conscious person, it's important to seek out and assess your own definition of success in order to build stepping stones toward a life desired and fully lived. This of course is a work in progress, but having a defined and clear blueprint to grow and to operate your own personal life is the starting point for success.

John Wooden (October 14, 1910 - June 04, 2010), the legendary hall of fame college basketball coach, has assessed and declared his own definition of success. When he said, "Success is peace of mind that is a direct result of self-satisfaction in knowing you have given your best effort to become the best of which you are capable," Coach Wooden is best known for his positive example as a person of character. Even though he coached basketball in high school and college for over forty years and had only one losing season (his first). His focus on developing good character and citizenship in young men had a far reaching impact. In the twenty-seven years as the coach of the UCLA Bruins Basketball Program, he never used the word "winning!" His leadership led his UCLA teams to four undefeated seasons and a record of ten NCAA championships (including seven in a row), completely unheard of in the modern world of athletics. He put his energy on what could be controlled and let go of what couldn't. He used basketball to teach his players the principles of a successful life. He sought his own clarity and defined success for himself and lived it. The basketball scoreboard did not define his philosophy of success, he believed in giving the very best a person could possibly give, and then success, in winning, was, and is, a by-product. If you were to pick a model for success, Mr. Wooden's vision of success ranks high.

Mary Kay Ash (1918-2002) is known as a champion for women. As an intelligent and determined single mother of three children she invested her savings of $5,000 and created a $2.8 billion dollar enterprise in beauty products. In pursuit of her own life purpose, she inspired and created business opportunities for thousands of women worldwide. Her organization, Mary Kay Cosmetics, Inc, stands as a replica for companies. She is known for rewarding her employees and especially top sales directors with a pink Cadillac. She models her philosophy, daily applying the golden rule, as she calls it. That is, to "treat everyone with respect." Mary Kay Ash states, "My definition of success would include living a balanced life. Balance means advancing your career up to, but not past, the point where it interferes with your happiness and relationships." Her definition of success was clear and she walked and talked her personal assessment of success. Her ways were a life-transforming example for the determined achiever to follow closely.

Anthony Robbins, the well-known author, motivational speaker, and performance coach has influenced millions of lives. He began his personal mission in life by founding the Robbins Research Institute at age twenty-five. He has created great opportunities and has become a wealthy man despite only graduating from high school. With a tremendous dose of personal passion and determination, he continues to be an influence for empowerment and personal development. Here is his definition of success as he states it in his book *Unlimited Power*: "To me success is the ongoing process of striving to become more. It is the opportunity to continually grow emotionally, socially, spiritually, physiologically, intellectually, and financially while contributing in some positive way to others." Mr. Robbins has outlined a clear, well thought out definition of success for his life. His representation of success is certainly an inspirational model for others to follow.

Ralph Waldo Emerson (1803-1882) was perhaps the most prolific and central figure of the American renaissance era. He was a preacher, lecturer, poet, and novelist, well known for his friendships and mentoring of some of the literary world's great authors and writers, including Nathaniel Hawthorne, Henry David Thoreau, and many others. Emerson was a man familiar with failure and personal pain. Losing his beloved wife, youngest son, and dearest brother to early deaths, he endured the challenges that hindered his promising career as a minister and was disheartened by a war that divided the country he loved. He trusted success and never gave up; he continued to believe in the greatest reason for his passion to succeed. His definition of success continues to inspire millions and gives evidence to how our personal definition comes from our views and experience in living.

> To laugh often and much;
> To win the respect of intelligent people
> And the affection of children,
> To earn the appreciation of honest critics
> And endure the betrayal of false friends;
> To appreciate beauty,
> To find the best in others,
> To leave the world a bit better
> Whether by a healthy child, a garden patch,
> Or a redeemed social condition;
> To know even one life has breathed easier
> Because you lived.
> This is to have succeeded.

Often our definition resonates in a deep place well within our spirit. Consider the last phrase: "To know even one life has breathed easier because you lived. This is to have succeeded." Wow! Could this be a worthwhile motivation to live fully and always seek success?

Each of these individuals in their own personal way exhibited common sense for uncommon success. Though at times life was difficult, challenging, and uncertain, they progressed through to reach a successful outcome based on their own assessment of life. They are ordinary people who have invested an extraordinary amount of being clear and specific in defining their own success. Dwight Bain, author of *Destination Success,* states, "It is absolutely critical to have a personal definition of success if you want to achieve it."

In all things the seeker of success is in a constant mindful state of acknowledging how to define success for themselves and their situation. It matters not if you are a parent, an employee, a couple, a boss, a student, an actor, or whatever. No matter our role, each of us must clearly and specifically assess what success is in order to have it and get more of it. The comic actress Lily Tomlin once said, "I always wanted to be somebody but I should have been more specific." Can you be more specific to get clarity regarding your definition of success and what it means in the various components of your life? Take the time to investigate because the bottom line is success without fulfillment will be failure. It could make the difference between a life fulfilled and a life dissatisfied or even tormented. As a success coach I constantly ask for definitions of success from my clients and my circle of influence. I've selected some definitions to share with you. According to these individuals success is:

- Peace of mind through daily balancing my life, which include family and work.

- Raising healthy children to be responsible as adults.

- Being independent financially to help myself and others

- A thoughtful journey of satisfying achievement in my professional life to enjoy my retirement years.

- What I've learned and what I've become because of not giving up.

- A long lasting loving and passionate marriage

- Fulfilling my life purpose or the accomplishment of my soul mission.

- Unfolding good virtues and a positive character so I can have a healthy conscience.

- A specific goal, achieved and purposeful discovery so I can contribute to the world.

- Constantly providing safety and security for my family.

There are as many definitions of success as there are people to define them. Whether we declare it, recognize it, or are experiencing it, everyone has a definition. It's possibly just waiting to come out. We must experiment, get in the game of life and fully live and search for our definition in order to express it outwardly.

My definition of success is:

- A clear sense of purpose and living a life of faith while on this earth.

- A loving and healthy family, including friends.

- A sense of fulfillment of my creative heart and mind through teaching, writing, and coaching.

- A passion to work at contributing positively and lovingly to others everyday.

- A strong intention on leaving a legacy of a powerful influence for the world at large.

- A mission to never, ever give up or let up.

As we mature, enter into different phases, and advance in wisdom our definition evolves. It becomes clearer and even more defined. What is your definition of success? Reflect on it. Spend time probing this concept whole heartedly. Write it out. Start with a bulleted list and later write out in sentence form with more details. Review your definition daily for 30 days. See how it transforms you and your life. Take initiative and take action living out your definition. These are the initial steps for the success seeker. We all want success, but to have it, you must first define it.

FIELD ACTIVITIES FROM YOUR SUCCESS COACH

Take action and answer the following three questions:

1. Name two people whom you would define as successful. Describe their beliefs, character, and contributions to the world. Determine if you would model after them.

2. What two initial steps can you take to begin your incredible journey of success? Put on paper your definition of success.

3. From your perspective, what two things would you recommend to other success seekers to journey deep into success?

1.2 Sweet Successes are Made of This

Nothing splendid has ever been achieved except by those who dared believe that something inside them was superior to circumstances.

— BRUCE BARTON

There are three kinds of people in the world: People who make things happen, people who watch things happen, and people who get to the end of their lives and say, "What happened?" Those who look back and say, "What happened?" often feel that somehow success has passed them by." In fact, success really didn't pass them by. What really happened was they failed to research or study the topic of success and apply to their lives. Contrary to popular views, success is not a secret. People who take the time to learn about success discover that it can be found within. Hopefully, they will realize they were born to succeed. We all are. It has been there all along. The ingredients of success are found within you, me, and all humans.

In July of 1776 on a bright sunny day in Philadelphia, 56 delegates including 70 year old Benjamin Franklin, John Adams and Thomas Jefferson, gathered to dialogue on various beliefs and to come up with an agreement. After completing this task the results were put on parchment and signed by all. It was the new nation's most cherished symbol: The Declaration of Independence.

"CONTRARY TO POPULAR VIEWS, SUCCESS IS NOT A SECRET. PEOPLE WHO TAKE THE TIME TO LEARN ABOUT SUCCESS DISCOVER THAT IT CAN BE FOUND WITHIN."

They declared that all people can and have the right to be successful. Everyone is equal and has the right to life, liberty, and the pursuit of happiness. That in it self is evidence to support the value of success. A belief that each person is capable and can claim their right to create success for their own individual selves: How great is that?

To strengthen our ability to acquire success we must strengthen our inner belief that we can succeed. Todd Duncan, author of *The Power to be Your Best*, stated, "The path is life. The vehicle is you. The fuel supply is your belief system, which is supported by the principles on which you build your life." We must create for ourselves over and over a strong and working mindset that success is achievable and it is within us. The well-known psychiatrist of the early 1900s, Alfred Adler, firmly believed in the inborn success of all humans. The field of professional and personal coaching grew out of Adler's various theories and principles of human development and success. His foundational philosophy was that people can succeed and can accomplish great things in life to help themselves, others, and our society advance. We must come from that place of belief that all are capable of success.

When we begin to acknowledge and understand that success is inborn, we then can take full advantage of our innate potential. We then begin to accomplish great things to positively impact our everyday lives and those around us. The vast majority of people have no grasp of how intelligent, how resourceful, how creative, how resilient, and how powerful they really are.

I've been inspired by the uplifting 1994 Inaugural speech by the first democratic President of South Africa, Nelson Mandela. As an activist lawyer he was sent to a death camp for 27 years without cause and freed at 71 years of age. He displayed no bitterness or anger toward those who falsely accused him. During those years of imprisonment he was pressed to compromise his core beliefs for freedom; he refused. A highly respectful person, he believes all humans have within them the seed of success. In his address to the people of South Africa he commented, "We ask ourselves who am I to be brilliant, gorgeous, talented, and fabulous? Actually, who are you not to be? You are a child of God."

Life is sacred. It is magnificent being alive and being a human being. There is a tremendous power within all people that enables great awareness, which leads to evolving development, which creates achievement and moves us to what we all want in the end: success! Claude Bristol, author of *TNT – The Power Within You*, writes, "The fact that people have been able to survive all these centuries in the struggle against all forms of life and in spite of the inhumanities of his fellow man is proof that he possesses superior powers within." There seems to be this built-in guidance system implanted in all of us that gives us the capability to be successful in living. We can find it in nature and in the animal kingdom. This inner success mechanism helps us with the ability to solve problems, to overcome the elements, to persevere and to triumph, to ponder great thoughts, to feel deep emotions, and to seek out and discover new horizons as we improve and continue to grow and evolve as people.

Could it be that all that has life is designed to succeed in its own special way? Could there be a specific DNA or inherent software within all human beings that pre-programs us for success? Could it be that success is expressed uniquely in each of us? Pablo Casals once said, "In the whole of recorded history, there will never be another such as you. Each of us is a miracle in uniqueness." We are all gifted and have special ways in which our success unfolds to contribute to ourselves, to others, and to the world. Another artist, famed dancer and choreographer Martha Graham, said, "You are unique. If you do not express who and what you are, the world will not have it."

Seventeen-year-old Jason McElwain from a town called Greece, New York, jumped up in surprise when his basketball coach called on him with only four minutes left to enter the last home game of the season. This was his very first time ever to enter a high school basketball game. Jason (or J-Mac as they called him) a slender teenager, received the pass, took the shot and missed badly on his first attempt, and then again. Suddenly, with the crowd yelling in support for Jason and the clock ticking, he shot and scored. Then he scored again! In fact, he kept getting the ball and he kept scoring. He scored six 3-pointers and one 2-pointer for a total of 20 points, making him the game's high scorer – and all that in only four minutes! The coach couldn't believe it; the crowd couldn't stop loving it. Jason was carried off the court like a hero by fans and teammates.

What's special about this? Well, Jason had a history of trying out for the basketball team each year, only to be cut from the team every time. He finally was asked to volunteer his junior year as a team manager. Jason has severe autism and suffers from learning disabilities. He lacks strength and coordination. However, he never stopped loving and playing basketball every opportunity he had. He was an instant celebrity with headlines across the country, and highlights of his feat were shown repeatedly on the news and sports channels. He was invited to the White House to spend time with President Bush; he appeared on the Oprah Winfrey show; and he won the 2006 ESPY award for the best moment in sports.

Since the discovery of Jason's disabilities at a young age, his parents had been concerned about his financial security, and his ability to hold down a job as an adult. Worry no longer: Columbia Pictures will begin production on a movie about the life of Jason, co-produced by NBA hall of famer Magic Johnson. Those four minutes of success have changed Jason's life forever. Jason said, "It's like, the sky's the limit." Success is instinctive, it's deep seated, it's inbred. Success shows no favoritism because it's inherent in us all.

Jason's story of success has enlarged the hope of many, especially those of us who are mentally, emotionally, or physically challenged. There is something about the human spirit. Just a moment or a sense of success can make a life change forever. How many times have we seen the deprived, the disadvantaged, the underdog that the odds makers predict to never make it find a way to succeed? Though it does require something from you, be it faith, passion, courage, intention, or other dimensions within. In the book the *DNA of Success,* author Jack Zufelt stated, "Success is not found somewhere out there. Success resides inside, for each of us. You already have what it takes to succeed in life. You were born with all you need."

As humans we have thousands of years of ongoing triumph and success. Cultures have been established throughout history and survived. Pyramids have been built. Humans have learned to fly and have walked on the moon. Science and technology have given us numerous contributions. The advancement of medicine has greatly helped us increase health and recovery and the natural process of healing and wellness. Even a newborn baby comes into the world with a contribution of success for their fellow humans just by its own umbilical cord from which stem cells can be harvested. Amazing.

Nature is a system of success. Just look out and see how the air, the rain, and the sunshine combine to transform the ground, the grass, the trees, the animals, and the insects. No human person designed this process, nor is there a magic wand, pill, or potion to conjure up this process of growth. When we believe we are designed for success, we expand our own personal position of empowerment, and a new paradigm of accomplishment has taken root within us.

In 1845, a literary writer named Henry David Thoreau cleared out a wooded area near Concord, Massachusetts, and built a hut for twenty-eight dollars and twelve cents next to a pond called Walden. He moved out and moved in not to be a hermit or to run away from the world but to deeply experience his own capabilities and discover how he could be self-sufficient and achieve personal success. While creating the most influential work of his life he discovered and wrote that, "Man was born to succeed, not to fail."

We are not meant to fail as human beings. Think about this: do you go to school to get "Fs," do you raise children to be delinquents, do you get married to plan a divorce, do you seek a career to get little pay or recognition? NO. We're designed for success; and even when we fall short, it can be a source for success. We exist to succeed; our creator has given us that gift.

A basic biology example demonstrates a lesson about success. A simple seed produces a plant with its natural elements to produce growth. It automatically pushes its roots down and its leaves up, and thereby achieves its desired success. This principle can be applied to people. With its natural elements of growth it produces an automatic mechanism with the ability to push upward, sprout out, and grow, thereby achieving success. To grow, to produce, to learn and accomplish is to be on the road to success. We are meant to become better and more improved everyday. The seeds of success are within and the only evidence of that seed sprouting is your development and personal growth. "Growth is the only evidence of Life," said John Henry Newman. We are not designed to be infants forever. The only direction besides death is onward and upward and continual growth. Once we believe we are designed for maximum success, our own level of effectiveness increases. The personal power to achieve, accomplish, and create is within every person's capability; however, you must choose to believe that this is true and cultivate that belief to help it flourish even more.

William Glasser, M.D., author of *Choice Theory* promotes the philosophy of choice. He believes it is your choice that has created your reality. He states, "For all practical purposes, we choose everything we do, including the misery we experience." Our choices do matter — choose success. You do not need permission to be successful; you only need to first choose to be successful. The initial step is a heart and mind sense of intention, then a commitment to choose to have and be a success in whatever way you uniquely define it. We each have the ability to control our choices and to choose to be a person of success. We can choose its direction, its frequency, its resolution, or we can choose not to. We are people highly capable of empowering our lives. Make a choice. We all have free will.

Choose what can be rather than what cannot be in order to direct yourself toward accomplishment. We can go to college, we can be courageous, we can start a business, we can have love, we can have peace, we can change, and we can be happy. There are really hundreds of choices for everyone to claim and individually make for success on a daily basis. Coach Ken Anderson, a baseball coach and a master motivator of his high school players and students, has a favorite mantra of inspiration for success. He would shout out loud, "You win or lose by how well you choose." He would motivate his players to choose to give it their all: "Choose one hundred percent of your effort," he would say. He would passionately repeat his words until they internalized the true meaning of the value of good choices. This concept transformed their mindset into successful results. The amazing part is that they began to sincerely restructure their thinking and became achievers on the sports field as well as in the academic classroom. Eventually acknowledging and utilizing the success you have within becomes real when you make a heart-driven and mind-centered decision to believe that success is inside of you. To know success it's important to accept that you possess all the components. The person who succeeds is the person who develops what is within them. Believe it, and make a choice. It's within.

FIELD ACTIVITIES FROM YOUR SUCCESS COACH:

Take action and answer the following three questions:

1. **Explain a time when you had the inner conviction that you were going to succeed. What was that like for you? What happened?**

2. **What areas of your life are you now pursuing for a successful outcome? What's holding you up? What action(s) is essential today?**

3. **What mantra can you create and repeat seven times daily for 21 days straight to help you choose to believe?**

1.3 Simply Self-Responsibility

"The willingness to accept responsibility for one's own life is the source from which self-respect springs."

—JOAN DIDION

It's one thing being irresponsible; it's another not taking responsibility. If you plan on being a success, consider self-responsibility first. Each person is the source or cause of his or her own success or failure. The Law of Responsibility points to you and states you are fully responsible for everything you are, everything you have, and everything you achieve. Your dreams, careers, education, life work, relationships, aspirations, goals, and endeavors belong to you and you only. Self-responsibility is a critical part in creating the outcomes of our lives. The wellspring of success sprouts forth when the one in pursuit of accomplishing success takes on, and is accountable for, the great and not-so-great of what happens. There are no greater spoken words than, "It's about me, I own it, and I am responsible. I will do whatever it takes to make it right because it is my responsibility."

Success has a price. Disappointments, rejections, and breakdowns will occur during our desired or intended steps toward success – that's just a part of life and living. Not everything is going to go your way. However, we must have the constant understanding of self-responsibility and stay far away from blame, victimization, justification, excuses, condemnation, or finding fault. Wayne Dyer, a popular author and speaker, once said, "All blame is a waste of time. No matter how much fault, if you find another, and regardless of how much you blame another, it will never change you." If you look closely at the word "responsibility," it can be broken down into two words: response and ability — thus, the ability to choose your response.

The opportunity for success is enhanced when we are mindful that responsibility is about us and nothing else. It requires that your awareness of a responsible mindset be amplified. In the book, *Be the Person You Want to Be* by John J. Emerick, Jr., he states:

> "The responsibility mindset is perhaps the most pervasive and most powerful of all mindsets. It asserts that you are responsible for your life. Your life, and everything in it, is the result of your action or inaction. This is the exact opposite of the victim mentality in which they blame others for their situation in life. Those who employ the victim mentality do not change their lives because they believe that others exert control over them. If you accept the responsibility mindset, you understand that you have created your life to be the way it is. Therefore you are empowered to make a difference."

If you have attempted something in your life that didn't get you the results or success you desired, say, "It was because of me, nothing or no one else but me. Self-responsibility is not easy. It will separate you from the pack."

To uncover your understanding of success you must first come to terms that you create your own outcomes. We each can take charge and un-create it and recreate or try it again. However, each level of creation is still our responsibility. Start by saying from start to finish: this is my doing. I'm the sole creator of my outcomes. I take responsibility. George Washington Carver once said, "Ninety percent of all failures come from people who have a habit of making excuses." We've all been there from time to time, the point is in order to be successful, don't go there. Not taking responsibility and excuse making is not a new societal issue. It has deep historical roots.

"IF YOU HAVE ATTEMPTED SOMETHING IN YOUR LIFE THAT DIDN'T GET YOU THE RESULTS OR SUCCESS YOU DESIRED, SAY, 'IT WAS BECAUSE OF ME, NOTHING OR NO ONE ELSE BUT ME.' SELF-RESPONSIBILITY IS NOT EASY. IT WILL SEPARATE YOU FROM THE PACK.'"

Early centuries of philosophical world views have influenced our current society on the subject of responsibility and the self. We often indirectly and unconsciously adhere to the ancestral thoughts and attitudes, which, if we haven't done our own inquiry, can be a deterrent to our own personal crusade for success. There are three main philosophical doctrines that impact our society at large. They are Relativism, Determinism, and Entitlement.

Relativism dates back to the later half of the fifth century with the emergence of an intellectual group called the Sophists. Their view was that morals, values, and situational approaches are not absolute, but are relative to the person holding them. Thus, a person can hold an argument or position according to his or her own ethics. The author, Richard Tarnas, *Passions of the Western Minds*, writes, "The Sophist believed it did not matter if man had no certain insight into the world outside him. He could know only the contents of his own mind – appearance rather then essences. The aim was to serve your own needs." In other words, right or wrong, it's whatever fits the situation for responsibility or not.

Determinism was popularized in the late eighteenth century. This is the view that our behaviors were pre-determined. That we created action and behaved in a specific manner because of causes outside of our control. Events and situations are determined for us therefore, we are not responsible for our responses to them. 1960s comedian Flip

Wilson made famous the saying "The devil made me do it." Well, I don't know if Flip himself was a Philosophy major or not, but that phrase beautifully illustrates determinist thinking, which has had a tremendous influence on our culture.

Entitlement had its roots in an earlier time. However, it is ever so prominent in our society today. Entitlement is the belief that we are due a specific title, benefit, position, or status simply of who we are. We do not need to earn it by work or effort. This state of mind places the responsibility on someone or something else to give to us because it's due to us. It enhances the belief that we don't have a responsibility to earn because it should just be given to us. Besides, it was ours all along.

These philosophies are very influential in our lives; however, they often go undetected. They seep into our character and hurt (rather then help) the individual seeking to be successful in life. Author and motivational speaker, Dennis Waitley, said, "There are two primary choices in life: to accept conditions as they exist, or to accept the responsibility for changing them." Self- responsibility is a high achiever's way of life and a source for all of his or her success or failures. There is a direct connection between taking responsibility and feeling a sense of control. The more you say, "I am responsible!" the more of an internal locus of control you develop. Your internal locus of control assists you in being in charge of your life versus being controlled by the external situations.

Imagine a society where people would take full, total, and complete responsibility with no excuses for anything in their own life. What would the repercussions look like? Nathaniel Branden, PhD and author of *Taking Responsibility*, states, "The practice of self responsibility begins with the recognition that I am ultimately responsible for my own existence; that no one else is here on earth to serve me, take care of me, or fill my needs; I am the owner of no one's life but my own."

Realizing that we ultimately are responsible is one of the greatest lessons we can learn and apply to our way of being. If you haven't learned the lesson of being a responsible person, it's not too late. Life will provide you with plenty of opportunities to get it right. When you are aware and affirm that you are responsible and a person who takes responsibility for your own life, that will set the stage for bringing order to your world. What an example for those who will follow in your footsteps of success.

FIELD ACTIVITIES FROM YOUR SUCCESS COACH:

Taking action on these exercises and center yourself on self-responsibility.

1. **Look over each statement carefully. Fill in the last four spaces. Follow this path of responsibility for your personal success.**

I am...

- Responsible for the choices I make or don't make

- Responsible for what I feel and all my emotions

- Responsible for becoming the best person I can be

- Responsible for my words and what I communicate

- Responsible for helping and improving my life

- Responsible for my treatment of self and others

- Responsible for my behaviors and actions

- Responsible for the friends, associates I choose

I am...

- Responsible for _____

- Responsible for _____

- Responsible for _____

- Responsible for _____

2. **Practice taking responsibility on a current situation in your life. For further development, write out this exercise.**

Exercise: Describe, Observe, Plan, Implement, Evaluate:

A. Describe: Be clear and describe a challenge in your life.

B. Observe: Where are you responsible? Observe your part and your role.

C. Plan: Create a plan: Write out a positive solution.

D. Implement: Put an action into effect today.

E. Evaluate: Check out the results carefully.

Chapter 1

SIX VIP'S for Success Seekers

Successful people know that:

1. Success is a beautiful thing. It is what you, me, and everyone is seeking in life.

2. Success is self-defined. It is different for all and within reach of every person.

3. Success is our inheritance. Know with certainty that you are created to succeed.

4. Success begins when we take responsibility for everything in our lives. Including the good and the not so good.

5. Success will depend on how you respond to opportunities in your life. Consistently place yourself in the path of possibilities.

6. Success is a choice. You win or lose by how you choose. Choose wisely.

Chapter Two
Step 2: Apply Wisdom for Your Flight

YOUR PERSONAL LEARNING AND EXPERIENCE WHEN INTEGRATED
INTELLIGENTLY BRINGS FORTH WISDOM. APPLIED WISDOM
IS NECESSARY FOR YOUR JOURNEY TOWARD SUCCESS.

Successful people know that wisdom is a prerequisite for total success. Wisdom is the highest and deepest level of understanding, knowledge, and insight. The path to wisdom is paved with life's many teachings, experiences, and personal development. If you are determined to seek success let it be known that sooner or later wisdom will confront you; it will call out your name. When that occurs, listen carefully. We are often tempted to rush toward the quick fixes, the fast bucks, the easiest approaches, and the slickest methods — but hold up, don't be fooled. There will be an opportunity for you to embrace wisdom so you can learn well. Take heed because there are no shortcuts to success. You've heard the old saying, "Rome wasn't built in a day." It's true. It takes time. And for the trip to be successful, timing is everything. If you succumb to the temptations, the outcome tends to be that you wind up back where you started from, the beginning. The

Law of Timing says that with wisdom and preparation we can seize the moment. We can avoid going down the wrong path or being deceived.

Invest the time to do some personal work, develop a strong interest in getting to know yourself. We make better decisions when we know our strengths and the areas in our life that need to be strengthened. When I begin my one-on-one client sessions, I start the conversation with a simple question: Specifically, what do you want? What is your agenda? What is the outcome you want for our work together? Getting clear on a well-formed outcome helps create a conscious force to move you into place for a result. It is an initial step to figuring out what you really want and what purpose is motivating you. One of the top ten most influential business books by Forbes magazine and a book I highly endorse for every home and office library is the international best seller *7 Habits of Highly Effective People.* The author, Stephen R. Covey, founder of Covey Leadership Center, now Franklin Covey, has been a warrior for self-improvement. He received the Fatherhood Award by the National Fatherhood Institute and was selected as one of *Time* magazine's 25 most influential Americans. This book is a personal and professional development manual. I use it and refer to it frequently, especially with my executive clients. If you are determined to apply success to every area of your life, seek out good resources to read and study. If applied to your personal and professional life you will see how the seven habits integrate powerfully into your routines which will assist your awareness, life development and eventual growth. To add to your tool kit of success let's review.

Here they are:

Habit 1: *Be Proactive-* step forward. Consciously choose the most effective action in any given situation, thereby increasing your success rate.

Habit 2: *Begin with the End in Mind-* Develop a clear mission or definition of what is and is not important to you.

Habit 3: *Put First Things First-* Gain a reputation for excellent follow-through and superior organizational skills by greatly increasing your ability to focus on your top priorities.

Habit 4: *Think Win-Win-* Easily share recognition and success without fear of diminished personal importance. Create effective, long-term relationships built on mutual respect.

Habit 5: *Seek First to Understand, Then to be Understood-* Develop effective communication skills that lead to greater influence and faster problem solving. Learn to listen for clarity while eliminating prejudices and the desire to prescribe.

Habit 6: *Synergize-* Value and celebrate differences and understand how they contribute to innovative and better solutions. Maximize opinions, perspectives, and backgrounds rather than feel threatened by them.

Habit 7: *Sharpen the Saw-* Maintain and increase your newfound effectiveness by continually renewing yourself mentally and physically.

— STEPHEN R. COVEY

Embrace the habits to see how they can deeply influence your thinking and lifestyle. To know what you want and seek how to get there, use habit 2: *begin with the end in mind*. Once you discover what you want, then get laser focus on your outcome. If possible, hire a professional or executive coach for greater assistance and accountability. Above all, be attentive to self management. Know with certainty how you are able to self-manage the areas of your life that will help you succeed. Understand carefully: if you do not manage your life, you end up being managed and success is not likely.

2.1 Who Are You?

"I know who I am; therefore I can,
and so I will . . . because I must!"

— ANTHONY TAYLOR

It was a winter morning and I was headed down a wet freeway to be on time for a presentation. I was speaking on stress management. I walked into a very packed, lively audience and shared strategies on reducing stress and improving their quality of life. After the event, a lady asked me about my psycho-therapy services. Her challenges were stress related and getting on a positive track to change her "out of control life," as she describe it. I handed her my business card and a few days later she called and made a counseling appointment. In our initial session one of the questions I had asked was, "What is important to you?" She eagerly reached into her purse and handed me a picture of a horse. I gazed at the beautiful horse. She had expressed how she nurtured her prize horse by spending lots of time with her, feeding her top grain foods and vitamins. She exercised her, washed and groomed her, as well as had a large financial investment. After our conversation about her horse I asked, "Now tell me about you, what is important for you to change?" She gazed out the window and said tearfully, "I don't know, I guess everything, I have a miserable life."

After hearing her story, her deep pain and the events, the choices, the beliefs, the "craziness," as she called it, concerning her difficult life journey, I was happy she was ready to make important changes for the better. In my work with people who desire to change and improve their lives I steer them in the direction of looking at themselves. I hold up the mirror and begin with getting them to see themselves, to know who they truly are, and what would bring them clarity to live a healthy life.

I remember driving home that night after a large and trying caseload and thinking particularly of the woman client with her horse. What went through my mind was how we live in a society that is not in touch with who we are; we don't know ourselves. It seems people take better care of their animals than they do their own lives. They spend more time, energy, money on getting to know and care for their pets, their possessions, or their property than they do seeking to know themselves and the true purpose of their life. Not that the care of animals or possessions or other items is not worthy of our attention – it obviously is. And yet it is true that only as people get to know themselves can their

> "WHAT WENT THROUGH MY MIND WAS HOW WE LIVE IN A SOCIETY THAT IS NOT IN TOUCH WITH WHO WE ARE; WE DON'T KNOW OURSELVES. IT SEEMS PEOPLE TAKE BETTER CARE OF THEIR ANIMALS THAN THEY DO THEIR OWN LIVES."

brains serve them as a sharp and efficient tool and their inner being functions clearly. You perform better when you know yourself! Self-knowledge is the proper starting place for success. To know success is to know yourself closely and intimately.

W. Clement Stone in *The Success System that Never Fails* states, "to know where you're going and to know how to get there, you must first and foremost know yourself." Be mindful and conscious of you; in other words, study yourself. The greatest asset you have is you. I recall my time as a young U.S. Marine Corps Corporal. I was sent to twelve weeks of non-commissioned officer's training school at Camp Pendleton in California. The theme of the leadership academy comes from the longstanding, time -tested and revered traditional leadership principles. Each candidate was assessed according to the eleven leader-ship principles and how well the candidates applied those principles. The very first leadership principle is: To know thyself and seek self-improvement. It all starts and ends with knowing thyself. Marcus Au-relius, a Roman emperor and philosopher once said, "Look well into thyself: there is a source of strength which will always spring up if you look there." To "know thyself" was what the early philosophers advo-cated and sought after. It began with questions that lead to exploring the essence of being human. The inquiry started with the big questions of life: "Who are you? Who are we? Why are we here?"

Asking those questions directs us to think at the exploratory level, which leads us to discover our own answers, which moves us to deeper stages of our own self-analysis. This could be the beginning of going beyond the surface and digging at the inner layers of our being. Just living daily on planet earth awakens us to develop a greater inner sub-stance, especially when we begin to care about our lives. This opens our hearts and minds to be introspective of our own being. The first recorded Philosopher Socrates, a Greek citizen from the city of Athens, who at 70 years old would rather drink the poison hemlock and die than deny his principles, was reported to have said and believed that, "The unexamined life is not worth living." It was expressed by Socrates as his statement of truth two thousand five hundred years ago. Could it still be relevant for us today? From my perspective, it is even more so today.

With many people, common reactions to the idea of knowing thyself are fear, avoidance, or denial. When it comes to exploring your personal identity and knowing deeper truths about who you are and what you're really like, it can be somewhat intimidating. It often brings up negative emotions. We don't like or appreciate the things we find out about who we really are. Getting to know "you" and studying yourself can be painful work, but is absolutely necessary for growth. Nothing worthwhile is ever easy. To draw close to success in your work life and your intimate life, it's important to learn more about you.

Discover what you love or would like to love. Know your strengths and things to improve on. Seek to know the good and positive qualities about you and gather information on what you directly want to change. Identify the roles you have as a person, your likes and dislikes, your moods, your philosophies, and what your true purpose on earth is to be. This means that you enter into the classroom of your inner psyche, which is the Greek word for soul. In other words, enter into your soul. If you believe life is about learning, what greater subject to learn about than you?

Gary Zukav, author and speaker, believes life really is a school. In fact, he coined the phrase — Earth School. In his book, *"Heart of the Soul,"* he says, "The Earth School has more classes than can be printed in a catalog. Studying a class seriously is more than reading, understanding, discussing, and writing. If you want to pass this class you need to look inside your self." Gary Zukav gives us a simple and insightful metaphor about passing the classes of life's challenges by looking inward to know yourself. Think about it, life certainly is a school and we have many opportunities to learn about who we are, especially from the many challenges that come our way. You will be in a place of great advantage when you understand what motivates you, what influences your emotions, what makes you do the things you do and how you can change those things that are self-destructive. I once heard a speaker use a catchy phrase, "The more you learn the more you earn." I took it to mean we learn about ourselves and earn self-knowledge, self-respect, love for self and others. And yes, could all this learning lead to financial earnings? Why not?

First, concentrate on the learning; an ever-helpful and empowering principle to live by. We all must take ownership and possess our own individual identity. We have greater congruency and live more successfully when we identify our identity. According to Stedman Graham, author of *You Can Make it Happen*, self-knowledge is where success begins. He calls it "Validating Your ID." He says it this way, "You can't open a bank account, drive a car, or even get on the airplane without valid ID. And you can believe this: it is very difficult to get on the path of success and reach your full potential unless you also first validate your identity by deciding exactly who you are and where you want to go." If only we could influence our educational system that true school is first about discovering who you are, connecting students with their identity and their purpose; then come the facts and figures.

Each person must be motivated to do their own personal self-study work. You certainly would benefit in a close, intimate relationship with a person who is whole and has done their work. The employer would also reap rewards with an employee who is mature and self-evolved. I believe we must take a season each year for self-evaluation. A personal study program and educational classes along with a mentor, sponsor, counselor, or coach to assist you in self-exploration is the most powerful and effective approach. You will become a stronger, healthier person if you spend a season of each year on your growth.

Organizations and employers inquire for my services to specifically train, coach, and assist their employees and executive staff in seeking greater levels of personal development so the workplace will be more productive. Team building, anger management, cultural diversity, sexual harassment, communications, and violence in the workplace are but a few hot training topics in the corporate world. Let schooling and personal growth never end. Our personal life does affect our professional work and vice versa.

There are many educational and personal self-study programs that help. A time-tested program that is available to everyone and a system for growth that, when applied, brings forth change is the traditional Twelve-Step Program. The model of these steps throughout the years has helped thousands, even millions, of individuals looking to restore a sense of clarity and serenity to their lives. The original co-founder, Bill Wilson, who *Time* magazine named as one of the 100 most important people of the 20th century, tried for years to find sobriety from his alcohol challenge, but could not and continued to struggle. His story was dramatized in the 1989 movie with James Woods and James Garner, called "My name is Bill W." In 1935 his idea of helping others so he could help himself led him to co-create the (non-professional) organization named Alcoholics Anonymous Group and used a Twelve-Step approach as its guide.

Working with leaders, corporate executives, other professionals, as well as those seeking life enrichment, I encourage application to a working self-growth program. It enhances the growth and ongoing development required for progress and success. We are creatures of habit and products of our environments. We often have victories and enjoy periods of wellness; however, our human tendency is to relapse into unproductive patterns of behaviors. There is tremendous value in the philosophy of the twelve steps. It could apply to anyone and for any unhealthy topic. It applies to anyone serious about development and growth, whether in the work place or personal life. Here is an outline of the program.

THE TWELVE STEPS FOR EVERYONE

STEP ONE

We admitted we were powerless over our separation from God — that our lives had become unmanageable.

STEP TWO

Came to believe that a power greater than ourselves could restore us to have clarity.

STEP THREE

Made a decision to turn our will and our lives over to the care of God as we have understanding.

STEP FOUR

Made a searching and fearless moral inventory of ourselves.

STEP FIVE

Admitted to God, to ourselves, and to another human being the exact nature of our challenges.

STEP SIX

Were entirely ready to have God remove all these challenges of character.

STEP SEVEN

Humbly asked God to remove our shortcomings.

STEP EIGHT

Made a list of all persons we had harmed and became willing to make amends to them all.

STEP NINE

Made direct amends to such people wherever possible, except when to do so would injure them or others.

STEP TEN

Continued to take personal inventory and, when we were wrong, promptly admitted it.

STEP ELEVEN

Sought through prayer and meditation to improve our conscious contact with God as we have understanding, praying only for knowledge of God's will for us and the power to carry that out.

STEP TWELVE

Having had a spiritual awakening as the result of these steps, we tried to carry this message to others, and to practice these principles in all our affairs.

You may find the concept beneficial. Know that the model expands to many areas of our lives, not just with addictive issues. The idea is to seek what works for you, make a commitment and practice it regularly and effectively. A particular helpful step geared toward knowing yourself and seeking self-knowledge is step four: "Make a searching and fearless moral inventory of ourselves." Bill Wilson acknowledged the significance of discovering who you are, and getting insights into your character. Doing an inventory helps you see yourself for who you really are. It would require a continual inventory for awareness and a searching for deeper knowledge of yourself because we are forever changing.

Self-knowledge is of great significance not only to you, but to everyone around you. Knowing who you are leads you to your values. What is important to you — your standards, beliefs and mission. We make decisions according to our values. It's a tremendous gift to you to know yourself. It does require a courageous and forthright step. For many, this is often the more difficult step; but for success, getting to know you is vital. Only you can determine if you are ready for this initial big surge of development on the journey of maximizing your success.

FIELD ACTIVITIES FROM YOUR SUCCESS COACH:

Take action on these items for success.

1. **For greater enlightenment in you, do this self-assessment. Who are you? It's vital to begin the journey of self-discovery. Look closely at your score, translate your findings and insight in a personal journal, and then take action for personal success.**

Who Are You?

Answer each question as thoughtfully and truthfully as possible.

1)   Do you have a strong sense of personal identity?

[ ] Yes   [ ] No   [ ] Not Sure

2)   Do you know your family history, culture, and background?

[ ] Yes   [ ] No   [ ] Not Sure

3)   Do you know what your own personal needs are?

[ ] Yes   [ ] No   [ ] Not Sure

4)   Do you consider yourself a highly valuable and important person?

[ ] Yes   [ ] No   [ ] Not Sure

5)   Do you have a sense of mission for your life?

[ ] Yes   [ ] No   [ ] Not Sure

6)   Do you feel you belong or have a significant place in this world?

[ ] Yes   [ ] No   [ ] Not Sure

7)   Do you love and have love in your life?

[ ] Yes   [ ] No   [ ] Not Sure

8)   Do you have a variety of positive interests and hobbies?

[ ] Yes   [ ] No   [ ] Not Sure

9)   Does your profession, career, or life work create greater meaning for your life?

[ ] Yes   [ ] No   [ ] Not Sure

10) Do you know and have clarity on your values?

[ ] Yes   [ ] No   [ ] Not Sure

11) Do you recognize and align with your life purpose?

[ ] Yes   [ ] No   [ ] Not Sure

12) Do you know how to ask for or seek what you want?

[ ] Yes   [ ] No   [ ] Not Sure

13) Do you consider a higher existence, power, or God?

[ ] Yes   [ ] No   [ ] Not Sure

14) Do you have awareness of your mental, emotional, and physical faculties?

[ ] Yes   [ ] No   [ ] Not Sure

15) Do you have a passion for seeking greater insights into who you are?

[ ] Yes   [ ] No   [ ] Not Sure

If you answered "Yes" to 13 or more of the above questions, you have a deeper and more enhanced understanding of who you are. Consider each "No" or "Not sure" answer as a need for greater self-awareness and personal examination.

2. Review the list of values. Successful people look at life through the lens of their values; what's important to them. From that list choose your top ten. Reduce to your most significant five. Circle the important three. From what is left (three) imagine you are in a small row boat, in order to be saved two values must be sent overboard. The one left in the boat with you is your highest value. Remember, from who you are come your values. Date and list your values in your journal. Keep record of your life.

VALUES

Abundance	Encouragement	Knowledge	Self-actualization
Achievement	Enjoyment	Leadership	Self-control
Adaptability	Enterprise	Learning	Sensibility
Adventure	Enthusiasm	Love	Simplicity
Affection	Excellence	Loyalty	Sincerity
Ambition	Faith	Mastery	Skillfulness
Assertiveness	Family	Maturity	Sociability
Authenticity	Fitness	Meticulousness	Spirituality
Balance	Flexibility	Modesty	Status
Beauty	Focus	Nurturance	Strength
Boldness	Forgiveness	Optimism	Success
Calmness	Freedom	Organization	Tact
Care and Concern	Friendliness	Originality	Talent
Career	Fulfillment	Partnership	Teamwork
Children	Generosity	Patience	Thankfulness
Compassion	Gentleness	Peace	Thoroughness
Competence	God	Perseverance	Tolerance
Confidence	Growth	Persistence	Tranquility
Consideration	Hard work	Politeness	Trustworthiness
Contentment	Happiness	Practicality	Understanding
Contribution	Health	Professionalism	Uniqueness
Cooperation	Honesty	Progress	Versatility
Courage	Hope	Prosperity	Victory
Creativity	Humility	Punctuality	Vigor
Dependability	Humor	Purposefulness	Warmth
Determination	Imagination	Quality	Wealth
Diligence	Independence	Relationships	Willpower
Discipline	Innovation	Resourcefulness	Wisdom
Education	Integrity	Respect	Youthfulness
Effectiveness	Intelligence	Responsibility	Zeal
Empathy	Joy	Satisfaction	
Energy	Kindness	Security	

2.2 I Can See for Miles

Faith is the ability to see the invisible
Believe in the incredible
Do the impossible.

— PAUL MONOGHAN- AUTHOR

We live in a world filled with many distractions which take up our time and our concentration which pulls us away from what is truly meaningful to us. Excessive distractions will eventually derail us from our intended purpose. We can only obtain our purpose through a single laser- sharp and steadfast focus. It is our own determined focus which, when repeatedly practiced, guides us in accomplishing what it is we truly want. The longer we sustain our focus, without distractions, the closer we get to our outcome. For success to evolve it must be a consistent and daily habit of a desired intention. Our focus helps us see into a deeper reality of our purpose. We are able to see far ahead when our focus is there.

According to the U.S. Census Bureau statistics give us some indication of what occupies much of our focus in our lives today. A year contains 8,760 hours; 3,518 of those hours will be sitting in front of a tube watching television, which adds up to five months out of the year. Another 41 days is accumulated listening to the radio, 165 hours each surfing the internet, listening to recorded music, and reading the newspaper. According to Nielsen Media Research, the average American home now has more television sets than people. I'm not insinuating that all this time is mindless entertainment; surely there is some instructional value. The point is to be aware of our focus, and what distracts us from getting what we want and accomplishing success. The things we repeatedly focus on create a magnet for our lives. A steadfast and consistent focus is the cement of success. It lays the foundation to build upon and provides a grip to hold onto. The purpose of focus is for us to establish a concentrated stable place so one can move forward with a visual target to achieve. A focus that doesn't waver eliminates the non-essentials and guides our determination on the indispensables, the absolutes, the necessities.

I am by nature a very curious person; I believe this is one thing that gives those in the people oriented professions passion about their work. A sense of discovery is an important quality to have or to develop if you are to excel in working with people. The astronaut John Glenn once said, "The one quality in an astronaut more powerful than any is curiosity." So it is in the people profession. I personally like to study people and learn what makes them blast off. I often ask people who have accomplished an extraordinary feat or who define themselves as achieving a higher level of growth or improvement what efforts have guided them toward their accomplishments? Rarely do I hear: "It was my ability to focus that guided me. It was my consistent focus. It was buckling down and getting focused." It doesn't seem like we give much mention to concentration or our ability to focus. Yet it is precisely that steadfast focus that eventually helps you acquire your success.

Most people don't focus on focusing. Could it be we just get on a roll and "Just Do It" like the popular commercial by Nike? We just keep on doing it until it becomes a part of us or second nature; maybe it's some unconscious thing. Some may call it muscle memory, or maybe its maturity over time. I believe it's a system of learning, or what the well-known Psychologist, Abraham Maslow, calls the levels of competence.

Levels of Competence

Unconscious Incompetence

You aren't consciously aware
that what you are doing
isn't getting you the **results you want.**

Conscious Incompetence

You still aren't getting
the results you want; however,
you are **now aware of that fact.**

Conscious Competence

You have made a conscious choice
to do it differently in order
to get the results you want,
and **IT'S WORKING!**

Unconscious Competence

It no longer takes a deliberate effort
or a conscious choice on your part.
The things you have learned
are now such a natural,
integrated part of you.
They happen
Naturally, gracefully, easily, and effectively.

— ABRAHAM MASLOW

We could save a lot of time if we would find where our focus is and where it would lead us. For a person determined to be successful, this is an initial move toward the flow of accomplishment. Get in touch with what it is you are focused on. You must be attentive and vigilant to be connected to your focus. Dr. Phil McGraw in his book *Life Strategies: Outlining the Ten Laws of Life.* He starts in Life Law number one, "you either get it or you don't." The strategy: be one who gets it. In other words wake up, be aware, be mindful, and be conscious of what you are doing. You certainly will discover that you'll "get it" when you're being watchful of your task at hand. Eventually your focus will force you to perform better. Your focus will bring you greater efficiency and enhance the levels of competence in your own life.

I've learned that when I'm determined to accomplish a goal, a specific task, or project, that is when my boundaries are set and I let others know I'm zeroed in — so look out. It is the only way to get completion; without setting boundaries you enable behaviors in yourself or others that will not lead you to what you want. Possibly it is that way for you, too. I view focus to be clarity of specific attention or refined thought to a defined outcome, or a center of concentration. It really comes down to concentration, which is the steady ability to stay the course. Napoleon Hill, author of *The Law of Success*, who in 1908 was assigned by the philanthropist steel baron Andrew Carnegie to unfold the secrets of what creates success, believed the "Magic Key" to success is focus and concentration. Consider some of the most influential achievers and you will discover a commitment to a fierce and laser-like focus on specific and defined outcomes. It doesn't matter if you're an employee, an athlete, a spouse, a student, or a parent — it all requires a steady focus in order to be successful.

> "CONSIDER SOME OF THE MOST INFLUENTIAL ACHIEVERS AND YOU WILL DISCOVER A COMMITMENT TO A FIERCE AND LASER-LIKE FOCUS ON SPECIFIC AND DEFINED OUTCOMES."

Because of parents' dedicated focus on the wellness of their son, a nineteen-year-old youth captured national headlines and has demonstrated the power of focus which is inspiring for all to witness. A young married couple named Patrick John and Patricia Hughes came together to share their love for each other, share their faith, and share their passion for music. On March 10th of 1988 in Louisville, Kentucky, they gave birth to their first child, a son they named Patrick Henry Hughes. They went on to have two more boys, Jesse and Cameron. The couple made a determination that their sons and their family would be their first priority. Their values prompted that focus which has encouraged and enabled their oldest son Patrick Henry to fulfill his dream and capture the hearts and the determined spirit of a nation, in spite of very difficult circumstances.

Patrick Henry was born with a rare genetic disorder that left him with no eyes and crippled, unable to straighten his arms or legs. The couple's priority was focused on the care and comfort of their son, and they discovered playing music seemed to bring calmness to baby Patrick Henry. Then, amazingly, at nine months old he began playing notes by ear on the piano and by two years old he was playing full songs. This all came forth just by his listening to the tune. In fourth grade he was playing the trumpet and later in early high school earned all state honors in band and chorus. He was soon known as a gifted musician as well as a wonderful and amazing youth.

He has now performed at Grand Ole Opry, the Kennedy Center in Washington D.C., and traveled to Italy and South America. He has his own CD that includes a range of classical music, show tunes, and one of his own songs. For Patrick Henry, with all his musical accomplishments even before his eighteenth birthday, he was now well known as a tremendous talent. What was next for Patrick Henry was college. He had a strong desire to keep learning and keep growing, and he wanted to be like all the other kids his age, so he enrolled at the University of

Louisville. His special gift was soon discovered, and the head band director encouraged him to join the University marching band. His parents wondered if this was something that was possible, what with his medical situation and condition.

Again, the couple focused on a solution and they found a way. With some modifications to Patrick Henry's wheelchair, some practice, and with Dad committed to working the graveyard shift at UPS so he could be there everyday at school to assist his son, Patrick Henry earned a spot as trumpet position number seven. During half time performance at the University of Louisville football games, his father would maneuver and choreograph each move with the entire marching band; he became his son's legs on the field. Patrick Henry, a straight A student, was the winner of the 2006 Disney's Wide World of Sports Spirit Award given each year by college football's most inspirational figure. His father calls his son his hero. It is an amazing heartfelt story. Through the power of focus we can accomplish many things and help others succeed in life's many challenging occurrences. To succeed it requires a steadfast focus. You too can be a hero or help influence a person to be a hero. Start with getting focused.

Tiger Woods, one of the most successful golfers in the world, has an unshakable ability to concentrate. His father, Earl, taught him at an early age the importance of being focused. He encouraged his son that in order to be successful you must have discipline and you must practice, practice, and practice even more. It seems to come smoothly, efficiently, and naturally to him now. He perfected his concentration and focus. Some seem to think he just gets all the lucky breaks. If you were to follow his career you would observe that this is a person with a focused eye on excellence.

The truth is that the most successful people create their own luck. They appear lucky because of their focus and intense preparation, which has put them in the right place at the right time with the wisdom to take advantage of the opportunity which lead to making great things happen. Darren Hardy, publisher of Success magazine and author of the "Compound Effect," believes in a complete formula of getting lucky, It is, **preparation** (personal growth) + **attitude** (belief mindset) + **opportunity** (a good thing coming your way) + **action** (doing something about it) = **getting lucky.** Successful people incorporate these steps for a complete formula of success. It is positioning yourself for all the great possibilities that will eventually come your way. The legendary golfer, Arnold Palmer often says, "the more I practice the luckier I get."

Jack Canfield, Mark Victor Hansen, and Les Hewitt in their book *The Power of Focus* stated that, "The #1 reason that stops people from getting what they want is a lack of focus. People who focus on what they want prosper. Those who don't, struggle." It doesn't get any simpler than that. Finding your focus through discovering and knowing what you want and staying the course is a smart building block for your future. You will create success in your business, your finances, your health, your family, your relationships, your spiritual life, and, above all, success within yourself. Whatever you're pursuing, if you desire to create a higher level of achievement, it will require your unconditional focus. Remember this very important point: you don't get what you want, you get what you focus upon, then you get that which you wanted. Like gravity, it's a universal law.

FIELD ACTIVITIES FROM YOUR SUCCESS COACH:

Take action for ongoing growth.

1. **To achieve a higher level of focus write out on a 3x5 card your answers to these following questions. They will assist you in determining your focus:**

   - What do I specifically want?

   - What or who can assist me in getting what I want?

   - When will I take my first step toward getting what I want?

   - How can I increase my focus to get what I want?

   - When will it be important enough for me to practice consistently for twenty-one days straight?

2. **To strengthen your outcome, seek two additional resources that can assist you with your focus.**

2.3 Haven't Got Time for the Pain

You are a product of your environment.
So choose the environment that will best develop you
toward your objective...
Are the things around you helping you toward success
Or are they holding you back?

—W. CLEMENT STONE

Self management is necessary for success. A person lacking self-management skills will put a strain on their life and on other people. Without possessing the skills and abilities of managing ourselves and the affairs of our lives we allow other things, situations, and other individuals to manage us. When we allow that to happen, we have lost total control of our true and authentic self. We lose our personal power and sense of self because we have given it away. With no personal power we would be spending too much time in unwanted pain.

I'm reminded of a couple I casually met and spoke with some years ago. We were in a friendly dialogue and I would ask a simple question to build greater familiarity, and each time the wife would assertively step in and answer the question for both. I would make attempts to ask the husband a question, and she would insert her answer for him. This occurred more than several times. I couldn't quite figure this one out. The husband, an intelligent and upright fella, just politely nodded his head in agreement. I then interjected and half jokingly asked the husband if he was willing to incline to respond to my questions. He said, "Yes, but why? My wife has the right answers for both of us."

I thought to myself, hmm, where's the passion behind this relationship? Where does he belong, because someone else has the power and is in the management position for his life? For the success-minded person this arrangement would not work. We must have a sense of assertiveness and be able to be in management of our own existence as we share our lives with others. Every individual must claim his or her own power and ability to manage unless there are unforeseen medical or other circumstances. If we give our self management up, someone will control us and take over. The results may not be what we eventually want. I teach a class at a community college called "Self-Management for Success." We often have a waiting list for that class. It's not a mystery that people everywhere want to learn what to manage and how to manage their life in a healthy and prosperous manner.

So, the question for the high achiever is about what to specifically manage. I believe there are many areas of our lives that need constant consideration for effective self-management. However, breaking it into specific, simple, workable components helps us find a state of equilibrium where we won't feel like we are lost and overwhelmed. Let's look at the essential "Self-Management for Success" approaches. You will find that each area of management integrates with the others. For greater success in managing for specific outcomes, concentrate on six areas to directly manage: **1. time, 2. stress, 3. money, 4. health, 5. relationships, 6. career.** These specific six items, when managed well, help us stay connected to our priorities and keep us on track for optimum success. Review your personal assessment in each of the six categories. Concentrate on where you are and on the success you desire most. Place the top three most in need of management first. Move toward management which includes implementing the tips that are provided to guide you for greater results.

Let's look closer at the **Six Self Management Components: Management Strategies**

Management Strategy One:

<u>Manage Your Time:</u> One of the most valuable resources in the world is time. If you squander it, you've wasted a precious resource. We start with managing time because it affects everything. Without sound understanding of time management and the principles to assist us, the other management components rise up to distress us. Once time is used, it can't be recovered. Time management is essential for everyone's success. We can neglect or just lose track of time, and before you realize it we have spun our wheels and gone nowhere, which leads to breakdown.

We all have in common 24 hours a day. How is it that many accomplish more great things with the same amount of time than others? Time management is really a total package of life management. If for some reason you are not getting the things accomplished that you most desire, let's look at what you're doing or not doing with your time. Procrastination is often a culprit. Some reasons for procrastination are fear, boredom, stress, and laziness. To combat procrastination, try writing a plan, make yourself accountable, consider assets versus liabilities, and get support through coaching or mentoring. Delegating is also very helpful for the person mindful of success. It saves you time to get other things done. Trust that others can do the job as well as you can. It is important that we manage our time; it will affect our ability to get things accomplished. When we get things accomplished it in turn leads to success.

Fill out this chart:

Procrastination is deadly for the success seeker. List what topic or area in your life you are procrastinating in. Identify reasons. Brainstorm strategies to end procrastination. Write the reward you will receive with breaking through procrastination. Use additional paper as necessary.

PROCRASTINATION

Procrastination (Area of life)	Reasons for Behavior	Strategies to combat procrastination	Rewards of breakthrough

Don't say you don't have enough time.
You have exactly the same minutes and
hours per day that were given to:
Helen Keller, Pasteur, Michelangelo, Mother Teresa,
Leonardo Da Vinci, Thomas Jefferson, and Albert Einstein.

— H. JACKSON BROWN

Four Top Time Management Tips:

1. Identify time and energy drainers and set boundaries.

2. Know your best peak energy time and accomplish the hardest tasks at that time.

3. Carry a watch and always have a calendar system.

4. Make a To-Do list daily and check things off when complete.

Time-Management Assessment

Look at the following list and check off those items that relate to you.

1. _____		I feel that I do not have enough time for my family, friends, and myself.
2. _____		I feel that I waste too much time.
3. _____		I find myself constantly rushing.
4. _____		I find that I do not have enough time to do the things I really enjoy.
5. _____		I find that I frequently miss deadlines or am late for appointments.

6. _____	I spend almost no time planning my day.
7. _____	I almost never work with some kind of prioritized "to do" list.
8. _____	I have difficulty saying no to others when they make demands on my time.
9. _____	I rarely delegate tasks and responsibilities.
10. _____	I find that I procrastinate too often.
11. _____	I don't have/use a calendar system.
12. _____	I don't have clear knowledge of my peak energy times.
13. _____	I have not taken a vacation in years.
14. _____	I spend a lot of time looking for stuff.
15. _____	I do not have/use a watch.

Checking off only a few of the items on this list suggests that your time management skills require just a minor tune-up. Checking off more than four suggests that your time management skills may be in need of a major overhaul. Implement your action plan with the insights you've obtained from this assessment and the four top time management tips. Seek further resources as needed.

Management Strategy Two:

<u>Manage Your Stress:</u> There are warning signs in life and for the committed person on the path of success: beware of stress, for stress is difficult to manage. In today's society the alarming increase in health problems related to stress is expressed in the phrase "living in the age of anxiety." We must learn life saving coping skills because stress is not to be overlooked. It could mean the difference between early illness and extended wellness. If you were to stroll through a cemetery I would bet the majority of those now gone still had at least ten or more years of life left in them. Stress if not managed can kill prematurely. It has a high cost on our ability to pursue success, which is why management is so necessary. Stress is a state of mind that is created when a person responds or reacts to the events caused by external sources. It leads to other breakdowns on the emotional level.

There are assets and liabilities concerning stress. High stress keeps the body and mind in a constant state of emergency. We all have stress and we all need some level of stress, but too much will break you down. Often stress is accumulative — it adds up over time. If not managed or monitored it will affect you psychologically and physiologically. Stress also has an effect on other emotions which cause further breakdowns. Stress will effect the other self management components of your life so it is imperative that we are mindful of our levels of stress and manage them well.

Four Less Stress Strategies:

1. Get plenty of support, rest, good nutrition, and exercise regularly.

2. Discard toxic relationships and lifestyles. Learn to say no and set clear limits and standards.

3. Think about your cup being half full versus half empty. Be Positive.

4. Slow down, monitor, and pace your life daily. Don't forget a medical check-up.

> *We all generate it*
> *But if you don't dispose of it properly*
> *it will pile up and take over your life.*
>
> — DANZAE PACE

Take the standard Life Event Stress Scale assessment and add up the score. This scale is used to determine where you are on the scale according to the events and the meaning you give these events over the last 12 months. If it's a high score notice where to increase management areas in your life; consider what actions to implement. Use the four less stress strategies to assist you. Seek resources as needed.

Life Event Stress Scale:

Assess carefully, in the past twelve months, which of the following *major life events* have taken place in your life?

- Make a check mark next to each event that you have experienced this year.

- When complete, add up the points for each event.

- Calculate your score and review the scale.

- Implement the less-stress strategies for wellness.

Event	Stress Scores
___ Death of spouse	100
___ Divorce	73
___ Marital separation	65
___ Jail term	63
___ Death of a close family member	63
___ Personal injury or illness	53
___ Marriage	50
___ Fired from work	47
___ Marital reconciliation	45
___ Retirement	45
___ Change in family member's health	44
___ Pregnancy	40
___ Sex difficulties	39
___ Addition to family	39
___ Business readjustment	39
___ Change in financial status	38
___ Death of close friend	37
___ Change to a different line of work	36
___ Change in number of marital arguments	35
___ Mortgage or loan over $10,000	31
___ Foreclosure of mortgage or loan	30
___ Change in work responsibilities	29
___ Trouble with in-laws	29
___ Outstanding personal achievement	28
___ Spouse begins or stops work	26
___ Starting or finishing school	26
___ Change in living conditions	25
___ Revision of personal habits	24
___ Trouble with boss	23

___	Change in work hours, conditions	20
___	Change in residence	20
___	Change in schools	20
___	Change in recreational habits	19
___	Change in church activities	18
___	Change in social activities	18
___	Mortgage or loan under $10,000	17
___	Change in sleeping habits	16
___	Change in number of family gatherings	15
___	Change in eating habits	15
___	Vacation	13
___	Christmas season	12
___	Minor violation of the law	11

CALCULATE   Your total score: _____

SCORE SCALE:

149-248   Low susceptibility to stress-related illness

249-299   Medium susceptibility to stress-related illness

300 and over   High susceptibility to stress-related illness. Be on the alert!

Observe your assessment. Be mindful; apply the strategies for less stress. Always seek further resources as needed.

Management Strategy Three:

<u>Manage Your Money:</u> There has never been more personal wealth in America than there is today. Yet, most struggle with money. One of the best books written on people who manage their money well is the book *The Millionaire Next Door* by Thomas J Stanley, PhD and William D Danko, PhD. You will learn that the wealthy bargain shop, drive used cars, are frugal and they allocate their money efficiently in ways to build wealth.

Ask these questions: How can I make the most of my money? What is the best attitude about money? How can I seek to be financially successful? Reflect on your answers. The management of our money is often one of our biggest life challenges. Taking stock of your financial life is necessary for success. It affects other areas of your life and if not managed well can lead to other breakdown symptoms: anger, worry, fear, criminal behavior, divorce. Financial experts claim that more than half of the people retiring after 40 years of work will be dependent on the government or family members to survive their senior years. Money matters do matter; there seems to be plenty for everyone — it's just a matter of management. We need to put the time into organizing our financial world so we have less stress in the long run. A working success formula would be the 10/10/80 rule. Contribute 10 % of your income to a worthy cause, save 10% of your income for your retirement, and live your life on 80% of your income. It is imperative to manage our money for it affects our way of developing our lifestyle, our ability to contribute, and our future.

Four Money Management Tips:

1. Focus on getting out of debt. Live and spend within your means. Be positive about money.

2. Budget and set up a financial filing system. Always know where your money is going.

3. Plan, contribute, save, and invest wisely for the future.

4. Take advantage of tax benefits and seek out good deals first.

There is a secret psychology to money.
Most people don't know about it.
That's why most people never become financially successful.
A lack of money is not the problem;
It is merely a symptom of what is going on inside you.

—T. HARV EKER

Money Management Assessment

Score yourself from 1 to 10 depending on how true the statement is for you.

1. _____	I have a healthy and productive belief about money. I'm Receiving what I know and believe I'm worth.
2. _____	I am responsible and never worry about having enough money to pay my bills or debts.
3. _____	I have a history of positive money flow. I've learned how to create wealth. I know how to manage money and I have a plan for growing more..
4. _____	I take advantage of all tax reduction, and save 10% of my income.
5. _____	I'm earning the income I need to live the lifestyle I really want and I'm smart when it comes to money matters.
6. _____	I do not spend more than I earn and live well within my means. I'm wise with managing my money.
7. _____	If I lost my job or financial means, I have at least 6 months of savings to draw upon.
8. _____	I study and educate myself on ways to achieve my financial destiny.
9. _____	I have a written action plan with specific goals for achieving financial security and independence.
10. _____	I contribute 10% to healthy causes and have a prosperity mindset with a positive expectancy.

Add the score: Very Positive management- 100-94

Good management: 93-87

Ok management: 86-80

Needs management: 79-70

Review your assessment carefully. Focus on the four money management tips to enhance your self management for greater life success. Seek further resources as needed.

Management Strategy Four:

Manage Your Health: People concerned about being successful develop healthy daily habits that help them grow, which in turn is an example of our all-around vibrant health. Good health helps you seize the moment, the day, and your life. It takes thoughtfulness. It also takes energy to stay healthy. The more energy you put into your health, the more energy you get for your life. I believe our health is our most precious commodity. Without our health, we have nothing. We must have a strong desire to manage our health because our daily output depends on it. That includes our mental, emotional, physical, and spiritual health. Really, it's our overall wellness.

In the early 1900s the average life span was around forty to fifty years old. In 2002 the average life span is late seventies, and today it's increasing. There are more people living in their 100s than ever before. If we are living longer health must be our priority and our responsibility in order to assure quality of life in our longevity. We can combat sickness and ill health. However, to have a higher level of health requires proactive approaches, like exercise, rest, eating well, and avoiding excessive drinking, smoking, or harmful behaviors. It's never too late to get healthy. Make a commitment to live well and live deep into your senior years. It's imperative. Decide now to be healthy. Just being healthy is an indication of success.

Four Health Tips:

1. Decide to live a positive lifestyle that associates with longevity.

2. Decide to stay active through exercise, read daily, and be a mentor of wisdom to others.

3. Decide on quality, not quantity. Seek new and creative ways to keep hope, love, and joy alive.

4. Decide to laugh, lighten up, and share good times with others.

The combination of exercise and sensible eating boosts your ability to relax, improves your muscle tone, aids digestion, and clears your mind..

—ZIG ZIGLAR

Managing Your Health Assessment

Score yourself from 1 to 10 depending on how true the statement is for you.

1. _____	I exercise for at least 40 minutes, three times a week.
2. _____	I'm rarely low on energy, or highly stressed.

3. _____	I drink plenty of water and eat foods I know are nourishing to my body and mind.
4. _____	I'm at my ideal weight and I'm confident about my self image.
5. _____	I do not have any self-destructive habits (smoking, excessive drinking, etc.).
6. _____	I get enough sleep each night to wake up feeling alert and refreshed.
7. _____	People often comment on how youthful, healthy, fit, and vibrant I look and act.
8. _____	I educate myself on issues which can affect my health (books, workshops, audio/video tapes).
9. _____	I make regular visits to health professionals (counselors, doctors, dentists, etc.).
10. _____	I associate with healthy people and invest in my health through a program of nutritional supplementation.

Add the score: Very Positive management- 100-94

Good management: 93-87

Ok management: 86-80

Needs management: 79-70

Observe your assessment. What areas need attention, take action. Focus on the four health tips for an initial step toward greater health for self management for success. Seek further resources as needed.

Management Strategy Five:

<u>Manage Your Relationships:</u> Successful people work at having and managing nourishing relationships; it's vitally important for success. "No person is an island to themselves," wrote John Donne. We need relationships to survive and thrive. With closeness to others, and appropriate and healthy relationships we experience lower rates of chronic diseases, accidents, and even psychological impairments. Poor management of relationships will literally kill you. We all have relationships of various levels, degrees and capacities. They all require special attention and effective management . We cannot treat each person the same because we are all diverse, but it's important to manage our relationships thoughtfully and respectfully. Consider our circle of influence. At the core is where we are. The second circle or layer is our closest and most significant relationships — our spouses or partners, our children, our families and close friends. Then there are our co-workers and others in the next layer, the third layer in the circle. We need to be aware of all layers of our complete circle of influence of relationships for wholeness and wellness.

Statistics show that people in satisfying relationships function at a higher level and experience more joy and increase the success frequency. In fact, scientific research shows that good relationships and friendships put our brains and bodies in an optimal state of function, says psychologist Daniel Goleman, author of *Social Intelligence.* That state is associated with positive emotions which help strengthen our immune system. Therefore we live longer and happier lives. If we are going to succeed at fostering high functioning relationships, look to be prudent in relating as well as being caring and respectful. Exhibit this way of being in all circles of influence. Relationship wellness is critical for the success seeker and even the overall evaluation of success in our lives. It is necessary to fully and successfully manage our relationships which in turn enhances our attitudes and our overall well-being.

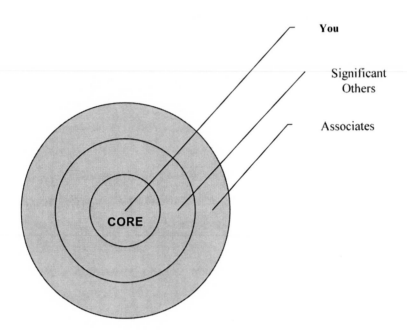

Four Steps for Managing Relationships:

1. Constantly develop and build on mutual respect and trust for one another.

2. Acknowledge feelings and ask what is needed. Make clear and concise requests.

3. Have a mutual give and receive approach. Say NO to relationships that are not kind and respectful.

4. Listen and communicate with uplifting language. Work to resolve all challenges effectively.

> *Personal relationships are the fertile soil*
> *from which all advancement, all success, all achievement*
> *in real life grow.*
>
> —BEN STEIN

Managing Your Relationships Assessment

Score yourself from 1 to 10 depending on how true the statement is for you.

1. _____	I feel happy in my relationships. No negative emotions -- like anger, jealousy, or resentment toward anyone in my life.
2. _____	I enjoy my relationships because they are healthy. I have quality time with my family, friends, and coworkers.
3. _____	It's not often that I feel lonely, isolated, confused or that nobody understands me.
4. _____	I have at least four close friends I can share my deepest thoughts and feelings with and am accepted for who I am.
5. _____	I support others and I have people who support and encourage me in the pursuit of my dreams, goals and pursuits.
6. _____	I communicate effectively, positively, and assertively to create WIN-WIN relationships.
7. _____	I give love and I feel loved by family, friends, and associates.

8. _____	A great deal of the time my relationships are a source of tremendous joy, laughter, and fulfillment.
9. _____	I'm a caring and optimistic person who sees the best in others.
10._____	I love people and I feel terrific about the relationships in my life.

Add the score: Very Positive management- 100-94

Good management: 93-87

Ok management: 86-80

Needs management: 79-70

Observe your assessment. Apply the four steps for managing relationships. Seek further resources as needed.

Management Strategy Six:

Manage Your Career: Success seekers are ever so mindful of their career path and their pursuit of their purpose. It is not a mystery that most people are highly unsatisfied when it comes to their career, jobs, or occupation. The truth is that a high percentage of people are stuck, unaware of what their capabilities are, what they want to do, or what their purpose is. A helpful approach is to think in terms of contribution of earnings for life work fulfillment. Successful people place their work, whether employed or self employed, at a high position of importance, without neglecting family or upsetting life balance.

Navigating your life work and purpose requires careful reflection, experimentation, and time. Planning and honing in on your creative talents is important because we spend 40 or more hours in our workplace. In order to be joyful at work, it is necessary to manage your choices, your education, your commitments, and your attitude concerning your career. Most people go through seven or more career directions before a permanent direction is discovered. Tap into your most passionate self and determine if this is the work you wish to do; and if it is, give it your all to be successful. Seek support or a career and transition coach to help you move in the right direction. Your occupation and career is one of the most important parts of your life and centers around one of the most significant decisions you will make. It is imperative to manage your career; it affects your time, stress, money, health, relationships, and all other levels of life satisfaction and purpose. Manage it well.

Four Workable Tips:

1. **Be patient but persistent in your desire for your greatest career fulfillment.**

2. **Be informed and be aware of all your possibilities and potential. Add to your qualifications and your strengths for employment.**

3. **Always know you're always working for yourself. You determine your destination.**

4. **Act like a leader and send the message that you know where you are going.**

*Genius is one percent inspiration
and ninety-nine percent perspiration.*
—THOMAS EDISON

Manage Your Career/Life Work Assessment

Score yourself from 1 to 10 depending on how true the statement is for you.

1. _____	I bring passion to my career because I love what I do for work.
2. _____	I respect the people I work with. They sincerely want success for me and our mission.
3. _____	I have written long- and short term goals for my career and life work.
4. _____	I'm using my skills, talents, and abilities to their fullest potential.
5. _____	The "sky's the limit" when it comes to career and earning opportunities.
6. _____	I have the support and skills necessary to advance to the position of my goals and dreams.
7. _____	I constantly engage in lifelong learning to better myself (books, audio/video tapes, seminars, and education classes)
8. _____	In my work people recognize my "CAN DO" attitude towards the challenges I face daily.

9. _____	Others recognize and reward my contributions.
10. _____	I experience a high level of fulfillment and satisfaction in my life work. I'm on purpose with my career.

Add the score: Very Positive management- 100-94

Good management: 93-87

Ok management: 86-80

Needs management: 79-70

Observe your assessment. Use the workable tips for assistance. Take other life circumstances into consideration. Be on purpose. Seek resources as needed.

FIELD ACTIVITIES FROM YOUR SUCCESS COACH:

Take action on these two recommendations.

1. **Review the six self-management strategies. Determine through the assessments areas that need your immediate attention. Write out a strategic approach to fill the gaps. Look at what needs to be self managed.**

2. **Find an accountability partner: a trusted friend, a mentor, a teacher, a co-worker. Collaborate and have a dialogue concerning the changes you will make in the next 30 days. Write up an accountability agreement, you and your partner sign it and allow yourself to be held accountable. Self management for success is serious business.**

Chapter Two

SIX VIP'S for Success Seekers

Successful people know that:

1. Success starts with self-knowledge, self-study and ongoing self-inventory. Never stop learning about yourself.

2. Success is associated with filling a need. Truly a successful person is one who finds a need and fills it.

3. Success is having the courage to enroll and show up for classes daily. Call it Earth School.

4. Success must be managed. It requires time, constant attention, steadfast concentration and laser-like focus

5. Success is unconscious competency — a consistent positive activity that comes naturally because of your life training.

6. Success is a state of equilibrium. It requires a strong self-management approach and balance to life.

Chapter Three
Step 3: Access Your Assets on the Quest

THE BEST WAY TO CONTRIBUTE TOWARD YOUR SUCCESS IS
TO TAP INTO ALL THAT IS WITHIN YOU. THAT INCLUDES
ALL THAT YOU HAVE AND ALL THAT YOU CAN BE.

Successful people know that true success happens from the inside, out. What you have stored up within you is vitally important. The Law of Correspondence says that our outer life is a reflection of our inner life. There is a direct link between your inner thoughts and feelings and the results you get. Being aware of how to access your internal resources to bring forth success is going to be very useful on the road of life toward accomplishment. We are gifted and skillful people and all our resources help us succeed. It is not so much the external resources that determine our success but rather it's the accumulation of all our internal life resources. We have the ability to access and reach the richness of our inner strength to help and guide us at anytime. That includes all of our experiences. The positive and the not-so-positive alike count as resources for us.

Webster's Dictionary describes the word "resource" as: *a source of support or help; an available supply; the ability to deal with a situation effectively.* What you have available to you is an internal system of support to move you forward to accomplish your outcome and to have the ability to deal with challenging situations effectively. It's all yours. It's an abundance of supplies that you have gathered internally during your sojourn on earth. Skills, tools, techniques, strategies, methods, application, or procedures that help us have the capacity to draw up and draw from our inner resources leading us to success.

Unfortunately, most people accumulate unhealthy thinking and beliefs which lead to poor results. However we can disregard distorted beliefs about ourselves and instead accumulate healthy attitudes that enhance us and influence our lifestyle. A key area to continually access is your most productive and positive view of yourself. For the majority of our population, we suffer from negativity which hinders our chances of success. Creative visualization is a tremendous tool to enrich your desire for success. Learning how to utilize the imagination can lead us and helps us achieve our life purpose. We all travel on the highway of life and within you is a gold mine of life treasures. Successful people know that it is a must to be able to dig deep and access personal treasures as well as visualize the success that will change their lives forever.

3.1 What's Self-Love Got to Do With It?

To attain "success" without attaining positive self-esteem is to be condemned to feeling like an imposter anxiously awaiting exposure.
—NATHANIEL BRANDON PhD

What is first and foremost one of the most important evaluations you will ever make in life? Could it be the evaluation you make of yourself? From my perspective, I believe it is. How we view our worth as a person affects how we think, how we feel, and how we behave. It has an outcome on how we connect and communicate with other people and eventually how our influence is determined. Self esteem is a particularly important matter for all humans. For the serious success seeker it is significant. Our whole world around us is impacted by our level of self-esteem. So, in asking successful people: What does Self Love got to do with it? The popular response has been, everything!

> "SO, IN ASKING SUCCESSFUL PEOPLE: WHAT DOES SELF LOVE GOT TO DO WITH IT? THE POPULAR RESPONSE HAS BEEN: EVERYTHING!"

What is self-esteem? Quite simply, I believe it is the healthy assertion that I like myself. I am valuable. I'm okay. I'm glad I'm me. The word "self" by definition is the complete and essential being of a person. The word "esteem" by definition is to regard with high respect. When I'm speaking of self-esteem I'm speaking of the healthy respect of myself. When we have healthy self-esteem it will greatly enhance our well-being as well as our interaction with others. People who have a good sense of self tend to respect and value the differences in others. Those without healthy views of themselves tend to disapprove of the difference of others. When you like yourself enough, Homer, the hostile co-worker, doesn't rattle your cage. When you like yourself enough, Curtis, the complaining customer, doesn't upset your meal time. When you like yourself enough, Denise, the demanding boss, doesn't affect your sleep routine. I'm not saying there won't be obstacles to be addressed, but with a healthy sense of self other people, events, or situations won't determine your sense of worth.

Our self-love is integral to our life purpose and destiny. Self-love, confidence, concept, and esteem are all interrelated distinctions that identify how we respect our human worth. I'm not sure if it has been determined if a healthy self is a prerequisite for success or success is a pre-requisite for developing a healthy self. Either way, it's necessary and vital to value who we are, to acknowledge our worth, and to love ourselves. Being comfortable in the space we take up is a major component of self love.

Two thousand years ago, one of the teachers of the Jewish Law who was considered an expert was looking to test Jesus of Nazareth. He asked Jesus what was the greatest commandment of the law? Jesus replied by saying, "Love the Lord God with all your heart, soul, and mind, and that you love your neighbor as yourself." (Mark 12: 30-31 NIV) Wow! That is possibly one of the greatest passages for all mankind. To love God, and to love people as yourself. To love your neighbor is a spiritual mandate and the foundation of the Golden Rule, but the phrase is not complete without the two words that follow, "as yourself." Yes, we are allowed to love ourselves. This is an important command, yet many struggle with self love, which sabotages living successfully.

You don't have to be a psychologist to know that the roots of poor self-esteem develop early in our lives and leave a negative imprint if we are not pro-active in self-care. Studies have determined that it is during the first seven years of our lives that we develop the majority of our personality, and many of us are still starving for life's most important need,— love. A top ten read for the success seeker is the book by M. Scott Peck *The Road Less Traveled.* In it he states, "It's been further suggested that the absence of love is the major cause of mental illness and that the presence of love is consequently the essential healing element." Be aware constantly that we need to be loved and give love for lasting health, wellness, and success.

From my understanding, it amazes me the volume and intensity of societal errors of modeling and teachings on love, especially self-love, which hurts individuals and eventually the human race as a whole. This will hinder our personal journey for success and the ability to accomplish. Let's examine three approaches to self-love: two very unhealthy approaches and how they hurt us and others, and then the one healthy approach that will move us confidently toward success. I call these three approaches "the good, the bad, and the ego."

The first I would like to discuss is the "ego," a destructive approach that models and teaches that self comes first, that what matters most is you. It communicates a message of arrogance, selfishness, and that it's all about me. It's a pattern of grandiosity with a high sense of self-importance. It puts your needs, wants, and desires before anyone or anything else. This type of self-love has a lack of empathy and violates the respect and rights of others. It seeks to win or come out on top while others lose. Egoists tell people exactly what they think, usually in excruciating details, and plan not just to win but to force others to admit defeat. They take a relentless aggressive stance on getting what they want at all cost. This can be linked to what is called narcissism. The term narcissism is derived from a Greek, myth. Narcissus was a handsome Greek youth who rejected the love advancement of the woodland spirit Echo. For punishment he was doomed to fall in love with his own reflection in a pool of water, later to be transformed to a flower. Narcissism is classified as a disorder in the DSM IV Psychological manual. In the final analysis this expression of self-love really says this person is suffering from a very fragile and distorted self-esteem. The egoist will eventually end up with a lack of love and support from others. Without inner transformation success is highly unlikely.

The second approach is the "bad." It models that self comes last. It communicates a message that others and their needs, wants, desires are more important, so we disregard ourselves. It is unhealthy, unwise, and unfulfilling in the end. The person with the "bad" view of self-love often exhibits passive traits, attitudes, and behaviors which lead to self-deprecating responses. "Baddies" are about denying themselves by displaying a way of being that is unclear, indecisive, and indirect. Their beliefs about themselves are lacking in importance, and they set poor limits and have distorted or no boundaries. They detest ego and believe that they are not ever to be selfish or self-centered. They hold the significance of others as greater than themselves. However this bad approach is too far the other way. This type of unhealthy love denies self. This poor sense of self-love means that others lose out on their creativity, contribution, and connection. In the final analysis this expression of self-love leads to low levels of emotional, mental, and physical health. This fragments our value and our aim for high self-esteem. Success is often not attainable without an awakening that leads to transformation.

This third approach of self-love is the "good." It is respectful to self and includes others. It is healthy, empowering, and leads toward ongoing success. It has a balance of give and take. It is assertive; it is pro-active, direct, and honest without harming someone else's sense of worth. This approach views their needs, wants, and desires as equal and important with those around them. It is being able to acknowledge and express their own feelings, as well as allowing others the same right. They value their personal autonomy. They work toward win-win outcomes. This self-love encourages a person to be collaborative and to enter into healthy relationships with clear boundaries. This self- love will add years to lives, as well as attracting more success throughout life. Obviously, this way of being will also have a profound effect on the world as a whole.

Being healthy is the well-being of sound mind, emotions, body and the inner soul. It is seeking a way to have total self acceptance. We accept ourselves and also accept the fact that no one is perfect in this world, including us. We are fully human and we are improving and getting better each waking day. It's an attitude of awareness of our abilities to acquire health. Healthy self-esteem adds greater joy to our living and increases our capacity to have success and share it with others.

Healthy self-esteem gives us greater ability to succeed in life.

Greater ability to:

- Overcome challenges effectively

- Be creative and use our imagination

- Access ambition and passion

- Laugh and have fun

- Identify nurturing relationships

- Trust others, and take risks

- Access courage and wisdom

- Respect other people

- Be happy and positive

- Love and experience intimacy

- Honor yourself

Begin to access those times when your esteem was high. What were you doing in your life? What did you believe? Who were your associates? Living a life of high self-esteem and autonomy is an ongoing process. However, the more you access productive thoughts and feelings about yourself, the more refined your sense of a healthy you becomes.

You grow stronger each day and you tend to ease up on being at war against yourself. You learn to have the ability to effectively increase your self-esteem and acknowledge your true and God give value as a special person. You have the ability to increase your confidence and self-esteem daily. Make honoring yourself a constant and important factor in your life – it's key in developing the success track you want to travel on for growth and empowerment.

FIELD EXERCISE FROM YOUR SUCCESS COACH:

Taking action will make these steps a reality in your life.

1. **Observe these tips. They promote a lifestyle of positive living and sound self-esteem. Circle the Top five that you want to begin to improve on immediately. Building a life of high self-esteem is a process. Move forward, one day at a time, for success.**

20 SUCCESS TIPS FOR SOUND SELF-ESTEEM

1. I accept faith over fear.	11. I do not lower myself on account of other's wealth or status.
2. I make decisions wisely and willingly accept the consequences.	12. I do not let people speak or treat me disrespectfully.
3. I set and achieve goals according to who I am and what I value.	13. I envision myself living a long, loving, and productive life.
4. I allow myself the freedom to make mistakes, learn, and grow.	14. I face reality honestly and let go of what I cannot change or control.
5. I train my mind by reading, attending classes, and studying to improve myself.	15. I keep myself fit, well-groomed, and present myself appropriately.
6. I choose healthy relationships and set clear boundaries.	16. I play; I have fun, and I have a variety of hobbies and interests.
7. I do not procrastinate or drift; I motivate myself in line with my chosen outcome.	17. I do not deny my needs, feelings, and opinions to please others.
8. I do not allow personal comparisons to affect my self-worth.	18. I have an orderly home.
9. I choose my occupation, lifestyle and living environment.	19. I share my love with family and friends and allow myself to receive.
10. I am authentic and true to my word.	20. I am enough.

2. A Self- Esteem Inventory:

A. Mental strength is crucial for self-acceptance. Commit to write and memorize daily motivational, devotional, and affirming statements, quotes or passages, to strengthen your mind.

B. Create a Self-Esteem Inventory. Brainstorm and write out a list of all the special gifts and talents you have. Include the positive qualities you like about yourself.

3.2 Imagine

What the mind can conceive and believe it can achieve.

— NAPOLEON HILL

A few years back a friend and successful businessman named Jerry used to meet with me a few times a week to work out at the gym. I was curious how he manifested success professionally. He would say, "I just help people visualize. Whether it's an abundance of business or life development or whatever. I guide people to fill in the blanks." Jerry often says that "creative vision is the art of seeing what is invisible, and making it visible, to the client." His motivation was to help business owners visualize their business in a place where they want it, even if it wasn't there yet. He would say, "Just pretend."

"NOTHING HAS EVER BEEN ESTABLISHED WITHOUT FIRST SEEING IT IN YOUR MIND'S EYE AND THEN FINDING A CREATIVE WAY TO BRING IT FORTH."

Visualization plays a major role in the attainment of success. Nothing has ever been established without first seeing it in your mind's eye and then finding a creative way to bring it forth. Visualization is the technique of utilizing our imagination to specifically create what we want for our future. Imagination is giving birth to an idea; it's manifesting a mental picture; it's accessing an image to create a reality or a different reality. Albert Einstein once said, "Imagination is more important than knowledge." Our imagination is powerful. In fact the great French dictator Napoleon Bonaparte said, "Imagination rules the world." There are no limits or boundaries to how far you would want to take your imagination. It works for all people, not just for some.

Henry David Thoreau knew the impact of an active imagination. He once said, "Go confidently in the direction of your dreams. Live the life you've imagined." All of the ways you want to be successful in start with your own imagination. As you create a vision or a mental picture, you cause a connection-like effect which aims you toward that mental picture or what you want.

Our ability to visualize and create mental pictures or images of what we would like our lives to be involves the flow of energy and information that form in our brain. We are always visualizing something because our subconscious mind and conscious mind are constantly at work. Scientific research of the working of the brain, or what is called Neurobiology, seeks to understand the mental biological reactions and its interactions with its target outcome. Also how tapping into the emotional control centers of the public brain helps us connect to our thoughts. The success seeker must have the insights into the inner working of the imagination. They must be determined to learn how to harness, manage, and control this mental power so they can achieve and get what truly is desired. Psychologists determined that our childhood experiences strongly influence our mental image, especially later as adults. Sigmund Freud, called the father of psychoanalysis, popularized this theory in the early stages of exploration of the discipline of Psychology.

Our mind is a fascinating muscle. Weighing less than five pounds, it comes with enormous capabilities. However, we use less then two percent of that capability. It's amazing how the mind can bring forth creative scenes and plant seeds for future success. It's the Law of sowing and reaping, which says as you put forth you will also get back. As you visualize, you shall see it come forth, much like a self-fulfilling prophecy.

There are two approaches for creative visualization. One is the *receptive* approach, where you exercise the flow of the imagination by allowing the impression to come to you. The second is the *active* approach, where you consciously choose what you wish to imagine and bring forth. In other words, you participate in the creation of your vision. Your own imagination opens the door to how you design your life. In the new *Psycho-Cybernetics* by Maxwell Maltz, M.D., he states, "You can not escape it. You will always act and perform and experience appropriate results in accordance with what you imagine to be true about yourself and your environment. This is a basic and fundamental law of the mind. It is the way we are built." Aristotle stated it clearly saying, "The soul...never thinks without a picture."

Speakers, sales people, top performers, athletes, are taught at every level a method called "mental rehearsal." Before you go into action, play the event over in your mind. See yourself performing the act successfully. Getting your total vision in alignment for your success will be determined in accordance with your ability to see it deep within. Since the beginning of time, men and women who have been known as high achievers and accomplished great success saw it in picture form, then rehearsed it for greater clarity, then gathered more information to create that reality. The more mental practice, the more you can reach for the attainment of the success you want. John F Kennedy, our 35th President, once used a quote from George Bernard Shaw that said, "Some see things and say 'Why?' but I dream of things that never were, and say 'Why not?'" The great dreamers and visionaries are familiar with the 'Why not?' phrase. Do you say, "Why not?"

Dan O'Neill was an inspired young man who said, "Why not?" He was an ambitious college graduate with an expanded imagination determined to be a contributor to the world. Early in his upbringing he had gone on several trips to remote parts of the world, and what he witnessed was the pain of poverty, hunger, war and destruction. He began to formulate ideas and soon had a plan for his vision. It started with him wanting to be a part of the solution for what could help make the world be a better place. In 1979 he gathered a small support group and organized a task force and responded to the plight of the Cambodian refugees fleeing from famine, war, and genocide of the "killing field." He called it, *Save the Refugees Fund*. This vision by Dan helped Americans see what can be done to help the world in crisis by providing relief assistance and life saving aid.

In 1982 the vision and work were expanded and the name was changed. Mercy Corps evolved, gaining national and international recognition for quick response, high impact, cost effective programs around the globe. Today, Mercy Corps has helped more than ten million people each year recover from disasters. From Somalia to Honduras, from Bosnia to New Orleans, wherever you find conflict or disaster, chances are you will find Mercy Corps. When sheepherders in Mongolia were faced with diminishing wool harvests, Mercy Corps taught them modern animal husbandry practices that increased the quantity of wool while reducing the effect on the environment. In Bosnia, Mercy Corps founded a financial services institution called Partner, which make loans to entrepreneurs, providing a source of funding for small- and medium-sized businesses. Mercy Corps took some of the best green practices in the Northwest and exported them to hurricane-battered New Orleans, where they have initiated a project to deconstruct rather than demolish older buildings so it can recycle and reuse the building materials. Mercy Corps workers help to build up communities to be stronger and more resilient. They work alongside to educate the community members and to find ways to solve their challenges of poverty and hunger. To help build schools, immunize children, and create a public health system.

Dan O'Neill used his vision and creative imagination to develop a program that allows a country to take action. Out of disaster and conflict emerge community and hope. He is inviting those who have the resources to make a contribution to what can be possible, to seek to be a part of the solution for the purpose of a healthier world. Dan travels and speaks at college campus, organizations, and special events, encouraging others to have a vision for a better way of assisting the world. He is asking "Why not?" you?

With imagination you cannot only create wonderful things in life; you can also imagine how long life (outside of fate or accidental incidences) will be for you or even live to survive tremendous obstacles. In fact, the understanding and importance of vision goes back three thousand years when Solomon, an ancient Hebrew king, considered one of the wisest men in history, was inspired to write, "Where there is no vision, the people perish (Proverbs 29:18)." Said another way, where we have no vision we lose our direction, our commitments, our creativity, our joy, sometimes even our will to live. Vision is essential for our very existence. Vicktor Frankl, a Jewish psychiatrist who was imprisoned in a Nazi concentration camp during World War II, knew the power of imagination. He visualized himself staying alive. He visualized seeing his wife again He visualized accomplishing his goal to get his first book published. Dr. Frankl saw firsthand that those who gave up hope, — who stopped their mental imagery of survival and only saw death all around — were not, in many cases, survivors. Because of his own ability to visualize and imagine possibilities beyond his circumstances, he is the author of the classic book, *Man's Search for Meaning*. To the question of "Should I continue to survive or should I die?" Viktor said, "Why not live?"

FIELD ACTIVITIES FROM YOUR SUCCESS COACH:

Take action on creating the life you want. Follow these two recommended exercises.

1. **A visualizing exercise. Let's examine a possible scenario: You're feeling lost and unproductive in life, including your career. A favorite part of your life is that you have a college degree and a positive network of friends and associates. Even so, you desire a higher quality of life and to change your career direction.**

    Let's begin to visualize. First, be mindful of your breath. Relax and be in a quiet meditative state. Start by imagining yourself in the highest quality of life that you probably can be in, even going for something beyond what seems possible now, if you want. It's to your liking. Imagine yourself utilizing your special gifts and talents. You access your life experience and your support network to move you into the life work you are most happy in. You see

yourself clearly in place. Imagine you're happy because you're living out your life purpose. You see yourself being grateful for the appreciation you are receiving for a job well done, and the financial compensation is rewarding. Add any other details that are significant to what you want. Seek to get a feeling in yourself that this is possible; experience it as if it were already happening in your life. Imagine that it is already so! How did it feel for you? Practice will help.

For you to get to the next step of success, take time, be still and exercise your mind. Take small steps toward creating mental pictures of how you want to develop in any area of your life. Visualization works, so begin to practice; you'll be surprised what shows up.

2. In detail write in your journal three things you've always dreamed of accomplishing. Observe what's present emotionally. Notice your physiological state of being.

3.3 Life is a Highway

Consult not your fears but your hopes and your dreams.
Think not about your frustrations, but
about your unfulfilled potential.
Concern yourself not with what you tried and failed
but with what is still possible for you to do.

— POPE JOHN XXIII

To reach various stages of success is like traveling on a highway. You put it in drive, step on the gas, and steer through the winding, sometimes hilly roads which are often long, maybe even treacherous. Yes, for those experienced travelers you are well aware of the many pit stops along the way. Life really is a highway and as we travel we accumulate many living experiences that are useful for seeking change or solutions to life's challenges. It's hard to realize that even the hard stuff that we go through can be useful in creating success. Our deep assets, inner resources, and accumulated personal experiences are important; and if we are able to recognize the value of our treasure deep within us, we can tap into its usefulness to help us when in doubt.

In the book *The Solution Focus: a simple way to positive change* by Paul Jackson and Mark McKergow, believes there is nothing we go through in life that should be wasted. They state that, "everything is a useful gift." The authors use the world's foremost medical hypnotist and one of the top ten most influential therapists of the past quarter century, according to the National Institute of Mental Health. Psychologist Dr. Milton Erickson is an example of a person who could utilize all that the client brings to a conversation as a useful tool for transformation. He would leave clients with a profound experience of self-discovery. He was the "master of utilization." He was constantly hypnotic, constantly therapeutic, and constantly teaching. His work pioneered the model of NLP (Neuro-linguistic Programming), a science of how the brain codes learning, language, and experience.

Erickson believed in using the process of our entire personal power that has been accumulated. He himself was keenly aware of the necessity to use all our human faculties for he personally was dyslexic, color blind, tone deaf, prone to vertigo, and plagued with polio at age 17 and again at 51. He spent his last 13 years in a wheelchair doing his greatest work as a therapist. His study of hypnosis taught him that altered mental states and trance were very much a part of daily functioning. He acknowledged that most of the rule of life prescribing human limitations were arbitrary concepts and beliefs, not facts.

Erickson's list of useful gifts included "all aspects of the patient or the environment. This includes both conscious and unconscious offerings, resources, strengths, experiences, abilities (or disabilities), relationships, attitudes, problems, symptoms, deficits, environment, vocations, hobbies, aversions, emotions…the list is endless, but the concept is simple. If it's part of the patient's life, it may be useful in achieving a therapeutic goal, and if the patient brings it, it's probably more potent than anything the therapist can introduce to the situation." (p. 58) This understanding guides the success seeker, especially when we are being challenged in accomplishing a goal. We can recall and utilize all of our life travels including the highs and the lows as a useful gift. We don't have to be a well-known psychologist to be able to tap into our inner resources, or inner treasures. It is at our disposal at any time.

Some time ago I worked at Kaiser Permanente in the Psycho Education department as a facilitator. I was teaching a class called, "Depression and Low Self-Esteem." We had an exercise called "finding your treasures." It was an exercise focused on acknowledging your life accomplishments, big or small. They include degrees, certificate, and letters of recommendations, creeds, or just any type of life experience that shows up on paper or trophy form.

We were sharing around the room, when a member of the class was asked to share her life treasures. She had difficulty acknowledging that she had any worthy treasures and that anything good has come out of her life experience, a common mindset for those feeling that their life lacks value. She was a high level manager for a company and lately has had difficulty with self-doubt, which has affected building positive relationships in her work department. I asked her questions concerning her current work environment and about her ability to be hired for the position she has had for the past ten years. I discovered that she had prior work experience in the field early in her apprentice years and had attended college and received her master's degree. I asked her if her college degree was displayed in her office. She said she took it down and put it away two years ago. I asked her if she would be willing to dust it off and put it back where she could see the degree and others could see when they entered her office. She didn't see the logic; however, she was willing to negotiate and agreed for one week.

The following week in class I noticed an assertive connection and full eye contact with this member of the class. Included was a bright smile and a different way of using her words. I asked her about her week and the experiment with the degree on the wall. She reported she had surprising positive results. I asked what took place. She reported she started to rekindle a feeling of accomplishment and connect to success, which she said she hasn't felt in a long time. She started to recall what abilities she had to overcome obstacles in order to get that degree, which sparked some confidence. She began to speak with co-workers with a sense of belonging and positive outlook. She even had several people who noticed the degree and dialogue about the school and her experience there. It made a difference. She was able to tap into her past where her resources and treasures are and utilize them for her success today.

> "IF WE DID IT ONCE, WE CAN DO IT AGAIN. WE CAN DRAW FROM OUR GROWTH FROM YESTERDAY AND BUILD FOR TODAY AND TOMORROW."

Even the bad can be good. It depends on how we look at it. We often disqualify our past achievements; however, they are useful possibly for the challenges we may be going through now. If we did it once, we can do it again. We can draw from our growth from yesterday and build for today and tomorrow. Our high school years got us a diploma. What did that teach us: how to get up and catch a bus every morning, make friendships, how to attend class on time, how to put a schedule together, etc. Let's look at a failed relationship, what are the treasures there? Look at purchasing your home, what are the treasures there? Look at getting fired from a job, what are the treasures there?

A one-time student and now a colleague discovered it was her internal assets, inner resources, and inward treasures that pulled her out of a difficult place in her life. Victoria was the eldest sibling and only girl of four kids in her family of origin. She was always popular, sociable, academically gifted; everything just seemed to come easy for Victoria. She went on to college and maintained high grades, accomplished goals, kept active, and had a fair amount of gentleman callers. She received her degree in the science field and had no problem landing her first job after graduation at Intel Corp. She was one of the few women in a popular male-dominant culture known for their technological and scientific minds. Victoria would often be seen sitting in meetings with Intel's CEO, Andy Grove, and other high officials. She soon married a handsome, attentive man and had a son and a set of twin girls. Life just seemed to be moving smoothly, prosperously, and positively for her.

Then, a defining period in her life appeared. It was 1999 when Victoria said she hit rock bottom. A series of losses were suddenly occurring. Her mother who was her best friend, lost her battle with cancer, her youngest daughter was suffering from seizures from an earlier vaccine which caused medical challenges, and the pressures of a corporate job became more intense. In addition, she was losing herself. She said for the first time in her life she felt alone with no recognition of a personal identity. She felt depressed, hopeless, and helpless; she was deep in the valley of gloom. After experiencing years of mountain top living, a shift of more than four years of feeling as low as she could go, she decided she had enough. "I want myself back but only better," she proclaimed. She made a decision to rediscover her own significance.

She started by looking within. Her treasures, which had been hidden over the last four years because of her state of being, now became her focal point. It was her personal mission to regain her sense of self. To regain it means she once had it, and it was now time to get it back. She sought professionals in the fields of life coaching, health care, mental health care, and spiritual care to assist her. She utilized her new learning to address, edit, and sometimes redirect her psychological inner noise or negative self talk that often threatened to pull her back into relapse. She replaced the gloom and the negative with the positive and working attributes she once had and was well known for.

She claimed that her inner work helped her look wider and deeper and connect her to the big picture of her life. She read books and sought classes for greater self-knowledge. She soon increased her confidence and discovered a tremendous will to succeed for the quality of living, not just quantity of life. She became fully present for the learning of each challenge without judgment. She established new functioning patterns, and was living now on positive intention. I spoke with Victoria on January 18th of 2007. She said, "Today is my birthday and I just turned 51." She began to get teary eyed, I said, "Well, Happy Birthday Victoria!" I wanted to say something encouraging thinking she felt sad for getting older. So I gently said, "It's not how old, it's how you feel, right Victoria?" She said, "no…no…It's not about me turning 51, I love it. It's that last year I turned 50 and I was given a surprise birthday party and 100 people showed up. I've come to realize how far I've come." She also claimed that it was the difficult things and the hard test she experienced that helped her realize she had inner resources, assets, and treasures within her. It was her strength that she didn't even know she had that helped her to survive the tough stuff.

Today, Victoria is a tremendous wellness coach for women, and working on her first published book. Victoria was able to pull from her inner life and recall the good. The abundance she gained from the times she experienced success, of which there were many. Those times live in our bones and nervous system — they don't go away. For her new life, just living purposefully helped her go to a higher level of wanting to create greater meaning for what her life is and could be about. The mountain tops and the valleys were there to help her realize that it all matters. She stated, "I wouldn't be where I am today without both."

I remember my first job after graduate school. I was hired as a psychotherapist at an EAP (Employee Assistance Program) company. I had a very difficult time with one of the owners of the organization and was fired eight months later. After what occurred, I realized that was the best thing that could have ever happened to me and my career. After that stressful experience, I made a decision never to work for another employer again and to make a searching inventory of myself and what I wanted. I sought skills from my past, reviewed my present skills, and determined what I needed for my future. I chose for myself that self-employment and entrepreneurship was the best and right fit for me.

I set out to create my life purpose and I reviewed closely all my learning and growing experiences, my accomplishments, my travels, my character traits, and my inner will in the presence of fear and uncertainty. It all helped me to continue to grow as an independent business owner. With accumulating my experiences and my will to succeed I wrote out a plan and stuck to it. I began taking additional classes, visit the library, began to network, sought out possibilities, and knocked at the doorstep of destiny. I learned to be a successful entrepreneur, independent worker and a business person. Opportunities opened up and I have never looked back.

I thank that owner for firing me. Sometimes things happen for a reason. It's just meant to be. It would even be fair to say, life is a test. That testing forced me to dig deep into my inner resources: my true self, my assets, my treasures. Although I've had my share of bumps in the road, I can say I've sped up a little and now I'm steering on the super highway. I'm living my life purpose and it's lead me to some incredible paths of success that I would never have imagined. I continue to accumulate resources for living and store up more inner treasures. I say this not to impress you but to impress upon you to get on the road. Travel life's highways. Accumulate and store up treasures. Stay in the driver's seat. You too will steer onto the super highway. I may see you on the road. Yes, life is a highway.

FIELD ACTIVITIES FROM YOUR SUCCESS COACH:

Taking action will make things happen. Recommend the following three exercises.

1. **Create your own personal treasure chest: Start to dust off your achievements. Treasure the positive recognition, the past awards, and the hard work of accomplishments. A personal treasure chest helps us to recall inner resources and strengths to restore a more positive perspective about ourselves, our situation, and our ability to triumph for the future.**

POSITIVE RECOGNITIONS COMES IN MANY FORMS:

- Awards
- Certificates
- Diplomas
- Degrees
- Recognition for a job well done
- Thank you notes and letters
- Greeting cards or sentiments
- Letters of recommendation
- Employer evaluations

- Written comments on assignments

- Creeds/deeds

2. Explore your surroundings for affirmations from your life — all the things you have earned from your efforts. Find a suitable container. Start accumulating, collecting, and building your own **PERSONAL TREASURE CHEST** and put it in a prominent place. Become familiar with recognizing your life's treasures, assets, and personal victories.

   List your treasures:

   -

   -

   -

   -

   -

3. Thoughtfully and tactfully display or share your accomplishments with others. Notice what occurs within you and the communication response of others.

Chapter Three

SIX VIP'S for Success Seekers

Successful people know that:

1. Success is constantly calling you to implement the command to love, including yourself.

2. Success is visualizing your best life and bringing it forward.

3. Success is when luck equals preparation, attitude, opportunity, and action.

4. Success is being resourceful. It is acknowledging all your life treasures that you have accumulated on life's highway.

5. Success is victory with yourself. It is recalling your inner assets when there is a challenge before you.

6. Success is contribution. It is saying, "Why not, me?"

Chapter Four
Step 4: Assemble Your Mentors for the Expedition

IF YOUR INFORMAL INFLUENCE ON OTHERS CREATES
MORE PRODUCTIVITY, MORE COMPETENCE, AND GREATER
GROWTH, SUCCESSFUL MENTORING HAS OCCURRED.

Successful people know that no one has ever made it to the top of their game without the help or guidance from others, either directly or indirectly. To a large extent, our lives are successful or not depending on the quality of our relationships. The student of success will always have his or her antennas up to observe and learn from other peoples' successes as well as from their mishaps. Mentoring is an integral part of maximizing your full potential. The impact of mentoring can be illustrated in the following story.

"In 1919, a man recovering from injuries suffered in the Great War in Europe rented a small apartment in Chicago. He chose the location for its proximity to the home of Sherwood Anderson, the famous author. Anderson had penned the widely praised novel *Winesburg, Ohio*, and was known for his willingness to help younger writers. The two men became fast friends and spent nearly every day together for two years. They shared meals, took long walks, and discussed the craft of writing late into the night. The younger man often brought samples of his work to Anderson, and the veteran author responded by giving brutally honest critiques. Yet the young writer was never deterred. Each time, he would listen, take careful notes, and then return to his typewriter to improve his material. He didn't try to defend himself, for, as he put it later, "I didn't know how to write until I met Sherwood Anderson." One of the most helpful things Anderson did for his young protégé was to introduce him to his network of associates in the publishing world. Soon, the younger man was writing on his own. In 1926, he published his first novel, which met with critical acclaim. Its title was *The Sun Also Rises,* and the author's name was Ernest Hemingway.

But wait! The story doesn't end there. After Hemingway left Chicago, Anderson moved to New Orleans. There he met another young wordsmith, a poet with an insatiable drive to improve his skills. Anderson put him through the same paces he had put Hemingway — writing, critiquing, discussing, encouraging — and always more writing. He gave the young man copies of his novels and encouraged him to read them carefully, noting the words, themes, and development of character and story. A year later, Anderson helped this man publish his first novel, *Soldier's Pay.* Three years later, this bright new talent, William Faulkner, produced *The Sound and the Fury,* and it quickly became an American masterpiece.

Anderson's role as a mentor to aspiring authors didn't end there. In California, he spent several years working with playwright Thomas Wolfe and a young man named John Steinbeck, among others. All tolled, three of Anderson's protégés earned Nobel Prizes and four Pulitzer Prizes for literature. The famous literary critic, Malcolm Cowley, said that Anderson was "the only writer of his generation to leave his mark on the style and vision of the next generation." What caused Anderson to so generously give of his time and expertise to help younger people? One reason might be that he himself had sat under the influence of an older writer, the great Theodore Dreiser. He also spent considerable time with Carl Sandburg. I find this pattern instructive. Not only does it mirror my own experience; it also illustrates what I have found to be a fundamental principle of human experience — that the greatest means of impacting the future is to build into another person's life. This process is called *mentoring*." (Chip McGregor)

Today, executives rely on mentors; businesses and entrepreneurs seek out mentors; leaders model after their mentors; and our kids need and must have good mentors. Mentors make a difference. I've had many mentors throughout my life; however, I often go back to honor a mentor who was foundational for me: my grandfather, Santiago James Velez. He modeled great love for God, for people, and for purposeful living. He believed in his calling to service for our fellow humans. He was a man that at 89 years old was held up at gunpoint as he walked for exercise in Central park in Manhattan, New York. He not only handed his wallet but volunteered his pocket change and watch. When asked why he did that he responded, "I can replace a watch and pocket change. Besides, I wanted to contribute some type of a blessing to that stranger." I was impacted by his many humane lessons and his contribution of great love; it has made a difference. He died peacefully at 98 years old. Successful people know that to capitalize on opportunities and create the life you desire, find a mentor.

4.1 I Go High With a Lotta Help from my Friends

The only gift is a portion of thyself
—RALPH WALDO EMERSON

Mentoring has been around for a long, long time. We can review lessons from the mentor of all mentors, Socrates, who mentored Plato, who mentored Aristotle, who mentored Alexander the Great, who.... you get the idea. We need mentors to help pass along success from person to person and one generation to the next. Isaac Newton once said "we stand on the shoulders of giants." I believe those giants he was referring to were our mentors from our past that helped us for our future. Take a close look at where you are in the way you do things, or the way you believe or view life. Chances are you had a person that modeled that way to you. That is how we learn, mature, grow, and develop. Other people have tremendous impacts on us that often last a lifetime. We often have to think hard or possibly don't remember who won the Nobel Peace Prize from two years ago, or who won Miss America in the year 2000, or the Academy Award for Best Female Performance of 2004, but we do remember the associates, the teachers, the school sports coaches, or the individuals who sincerely touched our inner spirit and had an influence on our minds and hearts.

One of the earliest references to mentoring can be found in Homer's story of *The Iliad*. When Odysseus, one of the wise Greek heroes, left home to fight in the war against the Trojans, he approached his trusted friend, named Mentor, and asked him to act as teacher and father to his son, Telemachus, while he was away. When young Telemachus wanted to learn the art of hunting, he spent time with Mentor. He watched and asked questions until his mentor believed the young man's skills were adequate to the task, after which he gave the boy the opportunity to hunt. It seemed if the story would continue the father would be pleased when returning because he found his son even better as a person because of mentor.

Duncan Campbell did not have pleasant memories of his childhood. In fact, he stated, "I was afraid, neglected, and raised myself." He managed to put himself through college, become a lawyer and later an entrepreneur. He made a promise once that if he had the financial resources he would help under privileged children have opportunities to succeed in life.

Duncan, in his relentless passion to help kids, researched the most effective way to impact a child. He discovered it was through the bond of mentoring for an extended period of time.

Well, in 1993 he made good on his promise, he personally funded 1.5 million dollars to start an organization that matched committed, fulltime mentors with impoverished kids and named it "Friends of the Children." The core of friends is the longevity and quality of the bond.

After ten years and thousands of children in the cities of New York, Seattle, Boston and Portland, Oregon, having the benefit of a mentor, according to the recent data, 85% graduated from high school, 90% avoided involvement in the juvenile system, and 95% avoided early unwed pregnancy, which are the three main goals at Friends of the Children. www.friendsofthechildren.org. In meeting Duncan, with his kind and gentle spirit you could only sense how important mentoring is to him. I will always remember his words, "I was born to be a friend."

Mentoring is really about Giving. Albert Einstein once said, "A successful man is one who receives a great deal from his fellow man, usually incomparably more than corresponds to his service to them. The value of a man, however, should be seen in what he gives and not in what he is able to receive." With personal attention, and a large dose of care and concern, it's giving of yourself for someone else's success. It's an informal way of serving for the greater good of the other person and eventually the world. One gives of his or her support, wisdom, and trust.

Mentors are positive contributors and exceptional examples to others. It comes from a deep sense of care to help others achieve their outcomes either personally or professionally. Mentoring is traveling alongside an individual to teach and train and then to pass it on. The model of mentoring has contributed much to working with people in the corporate world and in many areas of life, particularly the helping professions. Under the umbrella of the mentoring philosophy we can integrate with other helping approaches specifically what has now evolved into coaching.

Although the distinction of mentoring and professional and personal coaching has many similarities, they are also different. All successful athletes have been under the tutelage of a good mentor and coach. In the last decade, various skills from the court, the diamond, the rink, and the field have entered into the business world, the executive world, and the personal development world at somewhat of an expanded mental and emotional level. The concepts are similar to working with the individual client or with teams. Being in a formal professional relationship is important to the high achiever; a professional coach helps move the clients closer to their objective.

In a USA Today.com article from July 25, 2007 Karen Peterson wrote, "Personal growth is hot. Diagnosis is not. That is one reason America has seen a boom in the number of people offering services as a coach. These guides give clients the confidence to get unstuck- to change careers, repair relationships, or simply get their act together." So what is professional coaching? First, it is a partnership built on trust. It is specifically clarifying what the client wants and how they can obtain it through strategies, goals, and action approaches. The coach's main purpose is to assist a client through a skilled conversation and a thoughtful methodology. Coaching assists the individual toward assessing their own challenges, creating requests, brainstorming on what can be offered toward resolution and verbalizing declarations and initiate action steps to move forward to their desired outcome. It closes the gap between where you are and where you want to be.

> "SO WHAT IS PROFESSIONAL COACHING? FIRST, IT IS A PARTNERSHIP BUILD ON TRUST."

A coach assists people by:

- Focusing on their strengths and virtues

- Aligning them with their values, goals, and purpose

- Inquiry to help draw out inner resources for answers

- Supporting them to stay on track, and to be held accountable

- Enhancing clarity of their own vision and creativity

- Using solution language to address challenges

- Brainstorming action plans and strategizing goal setting

- Enhancing their motivation for performance and learning abilities

- Focusing on specific action steps to reach outcomes

- Addressing life balance issues in conversation.

- Bringing an individual to greater levels of personal awareness and self-knowledge

Being in partnership with a wise and skilled coach brings connection to your results. Purposeful outcomes come sooner and more effectively as you build for the future. A person lives more efficiently as they expand their future. People who hire a coach are seeking to excel, to accomplish, to succeed. Coaching helps individuals make specific and target changes. Coaching conversational topics include: clarity, purpose, leadership, transition, happiness, job issues, relationships, financial, pain, vision, passion, mastery, goals, integrity, creativity, abundance, future, balance, total growth and success.

MYTHS VS. TRUTH ABOUT COACHING:

1. **Myth:** *Focus on fixing people*

   Truth: Coaches operate from a philosophy that people are resourceful, whole, and capable. People don't need to be fixed. Coaches do not enable or rescue; they empower. Coaches are a champion for their people and co-create with their clients for their success.

2. **Myth:** *Focus on feedback*

Truth: Coaching requires that coaches master the art of asking powerful questions that lead clients or employees to their answers. The belief is that the answer is within. Coaches ask open-ended questions, empowering language, and methodologies to move clients toward outcomes. We teach people how to fish versus giving them a fish.

3. **Myth:** *Focus on feelings*

Truth: coaching is to deepen the learning both mentally and emotionally. People are multi-dimensional. We help individuals be wise and understand how to be emotionally intelligent. The process is for deep self-awareness and the creation of effective action steps for success.

4. **Myth:** *Focus on fu fu*

Truth: Education is paramount for the student of coaching. It is important that the prospective client ask where the coach got their training and/or certification. An academic school or program is best. The ICF is the governing body of all coaching schools. For a coach, knowing the core competencies of coaching from an ICF accredited school is vital. Coaching is a powerful language and methodology to be taught by professional teachers in the field. (http://www.coachfederation.org/ICF/)

5. **Myth:** *Focus on only financial gain*

Truth: Coaching is a calling for those who coach others. It is also a service. We call it being in the wisdom business. It's a business that brings individuals (serious about success) in alignment with what they are seeking. We work with people nationally and internationally. Coaches customize their services with their prospective clients. The phone and face to face are ways to bring our services forward. There is a large return on our investments for those that hire a seasoned coach.

Companies, organizations and the corporate environment have embraced the core competencies of coaching and the effectiveness it has on a workplace culture. Using the approach of coaching employees to higher levels of productivity has been a kinder, gentler way of getting employees to connect with the mission and have greater respect and harmony. Jack Canfield, author of *The Success Principle*, stated "of all things successful people do to accelerate their trip down the path to success, participating in some kind of coaching program is at the top of the list."

I believe psychotherapy is effective and needed for some people; however, therapy is not for everyone. I believe everyone could use and benefit from a powerful professional coach. I believe it enhances your ability to obtain and maintain success. In fact, I believe if we are serious about contributing to helping the world (which needs plenty of help) education and connection is the answer. That connection is through coaching a one-on-one conversation of empowerment. Education and coaching goes a long way for development and success.

I would go as far as believing that coaching has the potential to be a social transformer. That particularly is cause to have wise and passionate professionals doing this work. Coaching is especially acceptable to men who associate this approach to sports. It is also adolescent friendly which promotes a popularity in going to talk to your life coach or success coach. If you feel called to be in the people profession and would like to be certified there are specific training programs and schools that teach the principles and competences of coaching. Try it on for size; you never know how you can be a part of transforming for the better.

FIELD ACTIVITIES FROM YOUR SUCCESS COACH:

Take action on these four recommendations.

1. **Determine the specific area of your life for which you need a mentor or a coach.**

2. **Research and make a list of respectful people who express wisdom, care, and abilities in the areas you wish to succeed in.**

3. **Take action on follow up with a written request, proposal, or phone connection to begin your purposeful partnership for success.**

4. **Practice being a mentor yourself or seek to become a coach. Within the right circumstance talk to a person at work or a friend or an associate who has a challenge and volunteer to be a support. Use some of the information skills from this section. Notice your reaction to helping others.**

4.2 We are Community

"Anyone who imagines they can work alone
winds up surrounded by nothing but rivals.
The fact is others have to want you to succeed;
no one ascends alone."

—LANCE ARMSTRONG
SEVEN TIME TOUR DE FRANCE CHAMPION

In Latin, the derivative word for community is the "place where your gift is received." So, that assumes we all have gifts within us, and we are here to share our gifts. We do this in community. For the person who seeks success, you must be aware of how to create and cultivate community. Others must be able to receive your gifts and you must be able to receive the gifts of others; it helps to make the world go around. Whether we know it or not, we are always in a state of community. Albert Einstein wrote, "the individual, if left alone from birth, would remain primitive and beast-like in his thoughts and feelings to a degree that we can hardly conceive. The individual is what he is and has the significance that he has not so much in virtue of his individuality, but rather as a member of a great human community, which directs his material and spiritual existence from the cradle to the grave."

"WE NEED EACH OTHER, WE NEED COMMUNITY, WE NEED THE LEARNING, AND WE NEED THE RIGHT ASSOCIATES TO CONTINUE TO GROW AS A WHOLE."

We need each other, we need community, we need the learning, and we need the right associates to continue to grow as a whole. Some years ago I heard two political personalities have a heated debate, each seeing community from their perspective. One party said it takes a village to raise a child, the other party said it takes a family to raise a child. I'm not here to promote my political agenda but I believe it takes both. It takes a village. It's the community centers, the school system, the churches, the Boys and Girls Clubs, the libraries, and all the other developmental organizations that help all people young and old. It takes a responsible family (parents — mothers and fathers — grandparents, and extended family, including a significant loving caregiver or caretaker) with the ability to support, teach, and train within the family. We need both the village and the family.

Let's get clear on what a community is. A definition according to Webster's Dictionary community is:

- A united body of individuals

- A group of people with common characteristics or interest

- A group linked together by a common policy.

If I was to declare a theme in this definition, it would be a group of humans — more than one group, actually, with a feeling of unity among us all, having common traits, creating a bond, something that links us together. The truth is that people always have something to contribute to a community that can be shared with other members and serves as a healthy invitation for greater growth and success as a whole.

The building blocks of community would be a shared:

- Vision

- Mission

- Understanding

- Experience

- Resources

It has been said that Napoleon Hill's philosophy of success has produced more millionaires than any other credo in history. One of his Laws of Success is the establishment of the master mind concept. It simply is the bringing of two or more minds together harmoniously. The master mind group is the beginning of community; it just takes more than one person to formulate a group and it's a community. There are tremendous benefits in creating and cultivating a master mind group or a sense of community with others. Here are just a few benefits:

- A larger dimension of support, camaraderie, and a sense of belonging

- Enhance each member's individual progress

- Provide an opportunity to contribute on a greater scale (networking)

- Learn and grow from other members' thoughts and ideas

- It's more fun

We can discover that together is better. It provides a system of growth and support. It is in that support that we find growth and development. It helps people:

- Feel encouraged.

- Build confidence.

- Not be alone

- Recover from addictions/illness

- Live longer

- Go deep in learning

- Move forward

- Observe their lives

- Be coachable

- Enhance community

I was teaching a group of soon-to-be-certified coaches at "New Vibe Training." In the Professional Life Coaching curriculum there is a segment called the "enemies of community." I had a wonderful student who was a counselor from Israel upset with the word enemy; she felt there would not or should not be any enemies in a thriving community. I listened to her reasoning and invited other students to share. Soon many interesting aspects of debate centered on that topic. It concluded with a healthy reasoning together, as a community in class who could agree to disagree. We observed it would be ideal to always be in agreement and all be allies to have no enemies, however, we don't have a perfect world. Some forms of resistance or enemies bring establishments or communities down. Be alert, for it is important to not be naïve and passively identify those around you who do not wish you or your community well. Here is a list of four enemies that hamper the building of a thriving community:

1. *The Individualists*: People who isolate or hibernate. They put up a wall and don't share or let or want others to be a part of their lives. They disconnect and are withdrawn. Little if any contribution comes from a person set on being their own individualist.

2. *The Negativists*: People who are bitter and destructive with their attitudes. They tear down the positive and spread negative views

and attitudes onto others. Little if any contribution comes from a person set on being negative.

3. *The Egotists*: People who have an exaggerated sense of self-importance or are engrossed in themselves.. The self-absorbed individual disagrees with the fundamental purpose of community and creates conflict in a group. This personality hurts the bond necessary for growth. Little if any contribution comes from a person set on being conceited.

4. *The Gossipers*: People who participate in spreading rumors or hurtful talk of others. It's intended to be detrimental to another person's reputation. This single act hurts community members more than possibly any other act. Little if any contribution comes from a person set on being disrespectful by talking about others in a hurtful manner.

For the founder and director of the most successful urban youth program in the nation, Self Enhancement, Inc., in Portland, Oregon, community has been the cornerstone for Tony Hopson. His life mission was forged early from his neighborhood upbringing. It was the direct result of two components that inspired Tony years later to create and cultivate a spirit of community in his own hometown. It was the '60s and the civil rights movement was in full bloom. Those social incidents and societal concerns left a philosophical impact on the heart and mind of young Tony. He stated, "For people of color, community was a sense of survival; a place where people could identify with the struggles and connect with care and support. We felt safe together." The other ingredient was his sense of camaraderie and belonging that he received when the basketball team he played on won the 1972 State

High School Championship. He said, "It was that celebration of success and validation of relevance that brought a sense of unity to the entire inner city community."

Self Enhancement, Inc. is today the largest owned African-American-led non-profit entity that employs over 200 people from the community. It promotes hope for many young people ages 8 through 25, and provides services to families. Self Enhancement, Inc. serves kids within school programs, after-school programs, summer programs, and a charter school for sixth through eighth grades. Their organizational strengths are academics, the performing arts, and sports which helps SEI graduate 98% of its students and sends 80% to college. Tony knew at 13 years old when he was involved in his first camp for kids that he was meant to make a difference and that community was his playground. In 2007, Self-Enhancement Inc. celebrated their 25th anniversary and throughout the years their slogans have been, "Life has options" and "Youth Potential Realized." All this was possible because of the power of community.

If we were to view community primarily as a laboratory for life and character development, we would see the tremendous assets available to every person. All people — especially those in career professions — would gain greatly from knowing how to build and use community constructively and positively. The parents, the executives, the coaches, the leader, the pastor, the counselors, the sales person, the police officer, the teacher, the entrepreneur — all people from all professions and walks of life must learn the significance of community and how it helps us all to be successful.

FIELD ACTIVITIES FROM YOUR SUCCESS COACH:

Take action on these two items.

1. **Building a community that thrives. For greater success look to build community in your personal world. Be aware of how to establish and be in a thriving community. Complete this assessment.**

Please answer the following true/false questions and review your response.

True _____ False _____ 1. A thriving community can be established among any society or group of people.

True _____ False _____ 2. People build communities. An effective community is built with commonalities—mutual support, shared vision, goals, and members with positive attitudes.

True _____ False _____ 3. Knowing yourself, knowing what you want, your values and your roles are essential ingredients for a thriving community.

True _____ False _____ 4. Trust and respect are just minor factors in developing vital communities.

True _____ False _____ 5. Communities are successful when each member feels a personal sense of ownership.

True _____ False _____ 6. Community members should be more concerned with turf considerations than they are with having everyone work together for the greater good of all.

True _____ False _____ 7. Each community member is unique, special, and different. Input from all is important. Members are responsible for contributions.

True _____ False _____ 8. Conflict among community members is healthy if it is clearly identified, properly channeled, and quickly re-solved. Members can learn and grow from conflict.

True _____ False _____ 9. Community members who practice poor self-management and are lacking in self-discipline have no effect on the community.

True _____ False _____ 10.   Strong communities have members who are able to occupy various roles. Members can lead and members can follow. Recognizing roles and moving fluidly among them is useful in building a resilient community.

True _____ False _____ 11.   Successful communities have systems of recognition and reward. Acknowledgement matters.

True _____ False _____ 12.   Thriving communities are role models for other communities. Recognizing and using all the talents and gifts of community members make a community stronger.

If you marked nine of the above "True" you will very likely be success-ful in building a thriving community. You are a valuable asset as a com-munity member. Seek to endorse community for greater success.

2. **We all belong to a community. Observe your present community. List what two things you can do to make it better.**

4.3 Express Yourself

You have it easily in your power to increase the sum total of this world's happiness now. How? By giving a few words of sincere appreciation to someone who is lonely or discouraged. Perhaps you will forget tomorrow the kind words you say today, but the recipient may cherish them over a life time.

—DALE CARNEGIE

I will never forget a professor I had at Vanguard University in Southern California. He was one of the most popular teachers on campus. He became a professor in his fifties. He was in his sixties when I sat in his Psychology class. He daily came to class wearing a suit and tie and his Nike running shoes; only Dr. Grieves could get away with that. He had a bit of an Einstein look to him and was truly beloved by all his students. I remember he once said, "The more effective you are in communication, the better your people skills will be." Knowing how to effectively communicate helps you to get along with others. Our good people skills enhance our communication effectiveness as well as our effective communication enhances good people skills. They go hand in hand.

John Maxwell in his book *Winning with People* believes that having good people skills is the icing on the cake for success. He states, "All of life's successes come from initializing relationships with the right people and then strengthening those relationships by using good people skills. Likewise, life's failures can usually be traced back to people." The success-minded individual must be able to communicate well and demonstrate good people skills to establish and maintain relationships, both professionally and personally. A middle aged student who arrived early to the fall semester Communication class I was instructing at a community college approached me saying, "Please, please, teach me how to relate and get along with others. I just don't get this communication stuff and living with my parents is torture!"

Most individuals, young and old, feel just like that college student, desperate to learn how to relate. Human resource professionals estimate that 80% of the people who fail at their jobs do so for one main reason…they don't know how to relate well with others. It hurts to be in conflict with others. Since we live daily on this planet filled with humans, why not learn how to relate? Theodore Roosevelt once said, "The most important single ingredient in the formula of success is knowing how to get along with people." With a desire to study, to learn, and to observe how to be an effective and skilled communicator, one can achieve even the role of a master communicator. Think of the people you admired because of their abilities to communicate. They had developed their skill through practice. It didn't happen overnight. Your people skills will grow with time and practice. Find excellent communicators and model after them from your own way of being. We must learn to communicate well, because everything is connected to communication.

Psychologists have determined that nine times out of ten when we have a breakdown it can be traced to a breakdown in communication. That is why it is so important to learn communication strategies. The Latin word for communication is *communico* which means "to commune together." The word commune means to break bread together in harmony, to be in agreement, to share, to contemplate a related meaning. That meaning is motivation enough for me to want to do it more effectively. But what is communication? Communication is an art, it is self-expression, and it is a learned skill and a process of growth. It is also a science. It has a methodology to embrace.

I venture that it is also an exchange of ideas and information between people, both verbally and non-verbally, and the purpose is to attain a shared meaning. Meanings are in people first, then in words. We all interpret different meanings because we all have different temperaments, learning styles, and experiences. We also have different filters through which we receive the message or the meaning. We want to relate well and we want to do it in a way that brings everyone to a win-win resolution. For a chance to achieve harmonious relationships and lasting meaning we do it through mindful and intelligent communication approaches. To be successful we do this first by trying to see things the way the other person is seeing it, not the way we see it. That would mean building rapport. Rapport is walking alongside that person, having mutual understanding, camaraderie and interrelationship.

Abraham Lincoln once said, "If you would win a person over to your cause, first convince them to be your friend." I believe President Lincoln knew the importance of first having rapport with others in order to relate well. When you have rapport you get assistance, not resistance. Remember this, "The meaning of your communication is the response you get." So if you didn't get a desired response, perhaps it is not in the communication itself, but in the lack of rapport.

I have a favorite mantra that goes "Rapport will get you in the door." That is the essential component for people who connect. Rapport is built with trust. Ken Blanchard, the author of the book *Whale Done*, went to Orlando, Florida and visited Sea World. He witnessed Shamu the killer whale perform breathtaking stunts with his trainer. After the show, Blanchard approached the trainer and asked how he got this 9,000 pound whale to do these amazing acts. His reply, "the first six months all we do is spend time building a relationship of trust." He went on to say, "You don't want to be in a water tank with the most powerful predator on earth not trusting you."

Relationships can only flourish under the banner of trust. Building and maintaining the skill of rapport helps build trust. Other important people skills that develop from trust are listening. We feel important when we are listened to. Most people want to spend more time speaking, believing that speaking makes for great communication. Just the opposite. Psychologists researched CEO's of Fortune 500 companies for the most effective communication skill they possessed. The results were that several communication skills rated high, but the most effective was their ability to be pro-active and empathetic listeners. A good principle to remember is to listen pro-actively 80% of the time and speak only 20% of the time. Listening tells the other person you are interested in them. Dale Carnegie, the author of one of the most popular book in building people skill *How to win Friends and Influence People* written in 1936,, once said, "You can make more friends in two months by becoming interested in other people than you can in two years by trying to get people interested in you."

I once coached a client that was pro-active in finding a love partner to share her life. She was experimenting with e-harmony.com, an online dating service. She had an attractive profile and was receiving many requests. She had said that she admired many of the men, however, weighing through the various attributes made it difficult to choose. We worked together to compile important desired qualities and attributes and to work at narrowing it to two primary items that will help her get the love she wants. It was determined to closely observe communication style and delivery and people skills. Particularly how you are personally being treated. After a certain period of time she met a gentleman who had what she was looking for. They explored deeper levels of communication together and enjoyed how they respected and cared for one another. The last word I received, she was married to this person and soon to be a mother.

Recently, Harvard Business School did a study of the importance of "people skills" in business. After giving their M.B.A. graduates some tests to separate the students who had "good people skills" from those who did not, they followed these two groups of graduates for five years to see how they fared. They found that after five years, the graduates who ranked in the top 10 percent of the class in "people skills" were more successful and making 85 percent more money than the bottom 10 percent of the class in people skills! The researchers concluded that skills in relating and communicating to people were just as vital, or possibly even more valuable, than technical training.

Marshall B Roseberg, author of *Nonviolent Communication-A Language of Life,* believes your communication language can strengthen every area of your life even prevent conflicts and heal pain. Effective communication and good people skills really make a statement that says I really care about promoting the good will of people. I'm a people lover. I believe in the care to others. Psychologist and author, Virginia Satir illustrates the spirit of a language of life and nonviolent communication when she once said, "I want to appreciate you without judging. Join you without invading. Invite you without demanding. Leave you without guilt!" People who have enhanced the art and science of communication and do it well and utilize good people skills that accompany communication, enhance success everywhere they go. They leave a trail of people feeling empowered.

Sally Jewell was the jewel that Recreational Equipment Inc. (REI) in Kent, Washington, was looking for. Her ability to effectively communicate which lead to developing meaningful relationships in her world played a major role in being selected to lead the corporation, a consumer cooperative founded by local mountaineers in 1938. The company now has become the state's eighth largest private company and Sally is leading the way with her gifts of people development.

Born in England, Sally moved to the Seattle area in 1959. Ski lessons as a nine-year-old prompted her love for the outdoors, so connecting with this life work was a natural fit. Her colleagues said, "She is an interesting collection of strengths. Her engineering background provides her with strong technical and analytic skills, and, complemented by an incredible ability to connect with and motivate people, she has a winning combination. It is a classic, yet rare, combination of left-brain and right-brain skills," a long time colleague and friend said. She is warm and graceful. Despite her position, she is without pretense. She was offered and accepted a board seat in 1996, and four years later, the company offered her the position of chief operating officer.

Sally found plenty of struggles when she arrived. REI operated $11 million in the red on just under $700 million in sales. The retailer was having difficulty integrating its new online sales strategy with traditional catalog sales. Meanwhile, its retails stores needed maintenance. REI also had made a costly and unsuccessful attempt to establish a store in Japan. With Sally at the helm a turnaround strategy was now in place. REI closed its store in Japan, boosted catalog mailings and updated its retail stores and apparel. The strategy, which included freshening the look of REI's apparel and broadening REI's travel packages and product lines to appeal to less experienced and older outdoor enthusiasts, was a positive move.

During Sally's tenure as CEO, the company has added 35 stores, bringing the total to 89 stores in 25 states. The company increased its work force by about 30 percent to 8,451. Its active co-op membership jumped 76 percent to 3 million. In 2001, REI was $141 million in debt; it ended 2006 with $150 million in the positive. REI has joined the ranks of billion-dollar companies and was named to Fortune magazine "Best Companies to Work For" Hall of Fame. She has kept the company on a record-setting pace while taking bold steps to enhance REI's role as an environmental steward — all while continuing her community service on various boards, and using her master communication skills to produce results.

Sally has said, "Respect is key." She believes that to maintain a healthy corporate culture is to respect every employee's contribution to the company. It's a lesson she learned early on, when she was a young petroleum engineer at Mobil Oil, before it became Exxon Mobil Corp. She listens to people and has the ability to connect. She also hires well and inspires the sort of loyalty that makes people keep working with her. Her board and staff advisers admire the fact that, as strong as she is, she empowers other people which in turn helps grow the business as well as themselves. Sally Jewell's impeccable communication and excellent people skills along with keen business sense earned her the 2006 Puget Sound Business Journal's Executive of the Year award.

Pat Kilkenny would not be your traditional choice to lead an intercollegiate athletic department at one of the top universities in the country. In fact, former president, Dave Frohnmeyer, at the University of Oregon who hired Kilkenny, defended his choice after much public criticism. Why all the fuss? Mr. Kilkenny, a highly successful business man in the insurance industry was without an ounce of experience as an athletic director. To add to the unorthodox choice, he dropped out of college his senior year. This certainly gives credence to the phrase, "Only in America!" What makes Pat Kilkenny right for the job is what his business associates say — that he has the "golden touch." He has the gift of communicating well and working with people. People get motivated and want to work for and with him. He is skilled at bringing the best out in others. He claims he is even friends with people he has had to fire.

Pat Kilkenny says, "It is all about people." It is his effective communication approaches which translate to good people skills that transformed his executive position into acquiring revenue to purchase the insurance company he once worked for. His business vision and his goal toward expansion of niche insurance enhanced his company, Arrowhead General Insurance Agency, to $130 million annual revenue, and 500 employees. Associates and colleagues admired his ability to create team, bring energy, enhance creativity, and reach objectives. Pat went back to the University of Oregon where he started as a journalism major in 1970 and had a tremendous influence on the growth of the athletic department. He refused a salary and lead the charge in creating revenue through donors and other sources that built a new sports arena, the Matthew Knight arena, a new baseball stadium (named PK Park, his initials), and upgraded other sports complexes—as well as finding the time to complete his degree! If communicating well and having excellent people skills can influence growth and opportunities, just think how far, how long and how impactful your own golden touch can extend.

Twenty seven year old widower and mother, Ashley Smith from Atlanta, Georgia knows full well about the impact of the golden touch. Learning and communicating effectively along with developing her people skills especially her parenting influence were specific goals for her. On

March 11 of 2005 a man forced himself into Ashley's apartment and took her hostage. Brian Nichols had just escaped from Fulton County courthouse; he killed the judge and three others and stole a vehicle to get away. News coverage and a massive man hunt were widespread. Ashley, who was being held captive at gunpoint, began a purposeful conversation with her captor. Her words of hope, vision and purpose along with her ability to extend her knowledge of good people skills brought about a dynamic change of heart and mind to Mr. Nichols. After seven hours he surrendered peacefully to the authorities. Ashley declared her inspiration came from reading and studying and a determination on how to learn to be a better person. Specifically from a book called *The Purpose Driven Life*. She simply used words that communicated to Mr. Nichols purpose, no matter the situation. Her communication and people skills saved her life, his life, and possibly many others lives. In fact, her captor thought she was an angel from God.

> "SUCCESSFUL PEOPLE HAVE CONVERSATION POWER. THEY PLACE SKILLED COMMUNICATION AND A CARING AND REAL CONNECTION WITH PEOPLE HIGH ON THE LIST OF PERSONAL DEVELOPMENT PRIORITIES."

Communication is key for success. It's amazing how the words you say, how you say it, your timing, and your genuineness can bring about success in the most chaotic occurrences.

Successful people have conversation power. They place skilled communication and a caring and real connection with people high on the list of personal development priorities. They know it's about empowering language and words that make a difference.

This quote from Ancient Wisdom seems to sum it up when delivering the purpose of the golden touch. It's about planting seeds of effective communication and harvesting great people abilities which help people grow. It states:

> If you want one year of prosperity
> Grow grain;
> If you want ten years of prosperity
> Grow trees;
> If you want one hundred years of prosperity
> Grow people.

FIELD ACTIVITIES FROM YOUR SUCCESS COACH:

Take action on these three recommendations.

1. What are the three most important things you have learned about getting along and bring out the best in others?

2. Who are three people you would want to model after based on their excellent people and communication skills? Explain their qualities:

3. To enhance your conversation power what ways can you be more solution-focused than problem-focused in conversations?

Chapter Four

SIX VIP'S for Success Seekers

Successful people know that:

1. Success brings a purposeful connection to create higher levels of quality relationships.

2. Success seekers value people. They look for a sense of community to evolve and expand in.

3. Success is enhanced as you develop and mature your language and people skills.

4. Success happens with collaboration. It is the family and village working together to create a thriving community.

5. Success occurs with quality and commited mentors. It is teaching people how to fish so they can feast forever.

6. Success begets success. It produces a golden touch and a ripple effect.

Chapter Five
Step 5: Act to Catapult the Passage to Your Outcome

YOUR ATTITUDE ELEVATES YOUR ACTIONS OR KEEPS YOU
STUCK. ADAPTING A CAN-DO ATTITUDE, THEN TAKING
ACTION, IS A POSITIVE APPROACH TOWARD ACCOMPLISHMENT
AND NEVER GIVING UP ON YOUR DESIRED GOAL.

Successful people know that life rewards people of action. We cannot just talk about what we want — we must be willing to go and get it. Talk is cheap! Andrew Carnegie, at one time the richest man in the world, once said, "As I grow older, I pay less attention to what people say; I just watch what they do." The person with the go-get-it attitude and then actually goes into action to get it obtains the goal and the reward is success. My long time friend and former college roommate Mark Defazio owns a beautiful black Labrador retriever named Sadie. This is a dog that loves to run and be in the water, so living in Hawaii is ideal for both Mark and Sadie. They frequently visit the beach with Mark tossing Sadie's favorite chew toy and saying, "Go get it, Sadie go get it." She jubilantly springs into action with a determined attitude to go get it. She is rewarded with a treat for obtaining her goal. I am using this analogy to illustrate how important it is for the determined person to center in on a specific goal and go get it. That is a call to action for accomplishment. The Greek word for accomplish is the one which we derive our English word for energy. We must take action with plenty of energy to accomplish what we seek after. With this approach, your rewards will eventually follow.

In Siberia, a region of Eastern Russia, anxiety and fear governs the people, especially during the 1980s. One reason was the Chernobyl nuclear fall-out. The Sharapovas family sought to create opportunities for a healthy life and achievement for their young daughter Maria. They took action and left to the United States with seven hundred dollars in their pockets and an attitude of determination. They supported Maria's love and talent for playing tennis, so they sacrificed as a family and enrolled her in a famed Florida tennis academy for youngsters. With a willing attitude and a resolve to go after her goal she shocked the tennis world when at seventeen she upset the heavily favored Serena Williams to win the 2004 Wimbledon Tennis Championship. She had a go-get-it attitude and her spirited energy produced a tremendous accomplishment. You never know what great feat can be accomplished unless you are willing to get into the act.

The prime minister of England, Winston Churchill, was a central figure of leadership during World War II. It was a difficult and fearful time for the world at large. He once said, "I never worry about action, but only inaction." Being pro-active helps the process of you winning and getting what you want. "Action speaks louder than words" is a common saying, and it's true. Implementing your blueprint for success requires determined action. You cannot just think or talk about it; you must have a positive intention and make the effort, even if it's a small single step. Yoda, the old Jedi warrior in "The Empire Strikes Back," knows effective action quite well. He said, "You either do or you do not. There is no try." Great success is obtained by directing energy toward action that must be taken; a positive and right attitude will guide your launch off toward reaching your desired goal.

5.1 Attitude Is a Many Splendored Thing

A positive thinker does not refuse to recognize the negative,
he refuses to dwell on it.
Positive thinking is a form of thought which habitually
looks for the best results from the worst conditions.
—NORMAN VINCENT PEALE, 1898-1993

In 1879, a 43-year-old professor named Wilhelm Wundt at the University of Leipzig in Germany established something new to the world — a laboratory for the scientific study of the mind. It was a merging of philosophy and physiology that gave rise to what became Psychology. Wilhelm sought elements of consciousness of the mind and centered on the mind as a system of building blocks. Soon, another early pioneer in the field of psychology argued that the mind was not a thing but a process in which feelings and ideas formed a stream of consciousness. The theory was that the mind was fluid, alive, and moving. This was Dr. William James, known as the father of modern Psychology. He was an educator and philosopher who was interested in seeking his own wellness, so he created and taught a course at Harvard University called the Relations between Physiology and Psychology. Considered a brilliant mind, he later wrote one of the first publications of psychology called *The Principles of Psychology.* Dr. James once said one of the most important discoveries made by his generation was that by changing our attitudes we can change our lives.

That we can change our lives by first changing our attitude is now considered a major ingredient in transformation. Attitude is everything, and everything is about our attitude. Our initial thrust of attitude starts with how we think about our situation or events in our lives. I've often referred to a wisdom phrase in my teachings, "Life is between your ears; it's mental." It is how you deal with it at an attitude level. Our minds are like a computer. What we program into them determines how they will function. The most tech savvy computer ever made, programmed with the wrong software, will never function correctly. For instance, just like viruses in the cyber world that cause computer malfunctions, our mental computers are also susceptible to the data we put into it. If we choose to load up with bad data, it will limit how effective or successful we will be. Program yourself with the right attitude to receive the highest value of the things you're pursuing.

"Attitude is the source that fuels our altitude." I once stopped to ponder what that really meant. Then I discovered that when I changed my attitude with a particular challenge, I actually changed my ways. I've heard it said when you change the way you look at things, things change the way they look. This is true! As a person who wants more from living, one of the most important steps toward achieving your greatest potential is to learn how to monitor your attitude. It will certainly impact your measure of success in all areas of your life. Your attitude could be your best friend or your worst enemy. Although everyone has an attitude and displays it with various

> "ALTHOUGH EVERYONE HAS AN ATTITUDE AND DISPLAYS IT WITH VARIOUS EVENTS THAT OCCUR IN OUR LIVES, NOT EVERYONE HAS LEARNED TO HAVE THE ATTITUDE THAT BRINGS SUCCESS."

events that occur in our lives, not everyone has learned to have the attitude that brings success. It takes a lot of energy to be negative, and being positive in negative situations requires a lot of character work on our part.

Research has determined that people with a more positive attitude and greater optimism are more successful and live longer. Psychologist and Professor at the University of Pennsylvania, Dr. Martin Seligman, in 1999 was the incoming president of the APA (American Psychological Association). He wanted his year of reigning to focus on a specific theme that was to promote research on wellness and happiness. His mission was to identify what is right with people by accentuating the gifts of optimism, positive emotions, virtues, and healthy character traits. The psychology field knows plenty about depression, anxiety, hostility, obsessions, and neurosis. This new approach is called Positive Psychology and Dr. Seligman is known as the father of this movement. It is using a scientific method to understand the roots of virtues, strengths, and a good attitude, and how it enhances successful living.

It is a shift from pessimism to optimism that causes the prevention of breakdowns of the heart and mind. Positive Psychology is founded on the belief that people are competent, resourceful, capable, strong, and adequate that people want to be happy and lead meaningful and productive lives. People want to be able to cultivate the best within themselves. Positive Psychology is categorized in the six virtues: wisdom, courage, humanity, justice, temperance, and transcendence. In addition, is the list of 24 principle character strengths which lead to these virtues: creativity, curiosity, love, kindness, persistence, integrity, vitality, social intelligence, ethics, citizenship, fairness, leadership, love of learning, bravery, leadership, mercy, humility, prudence, perspective, hope, appreciation of beauty, humor, gratitude, and excellence.

The pursuit of happiness is not just a recent discourse. Over time, the great thinkers of humanity have sought to explore and explain this age old conversation concerning happiness. Philosophers like Aristotle said, "Happiness is an activity of the soul in conformity with excellence or virtue." Epictetus, the Greek stoic philosopher from the first century said, "Happiness begins with a clear understanding of one principle: what you can control and what you cannot." As we observe our society today, it seems there is a greater awareness and longing for happiness, even to a heightened degree. Happiness is attainable. Most of us know when we are not happy. Life is not very motivating, even uncomfortable at times. To attain it we must want it, we must decide to shift our lives, and reach out to find our individual path of happiness. To have happiness you, and only you, must be in charge of obtaining it. No one is in charge of your happiness nor can someone make you happy or be responsible for your happiness. It comes from being a driver, not a passenger on this journey toward happiness. Dan Baker, author of *What Happy People Know* believes people fall into traps that keep them from attaining their happiness. He lists the five traps of happiness.

Happiness Trap:

1. Trying to buy happiness

2. Trying to find happiness through pleasure

3. Trying to be happy by resolving the past

4. Trying to be happy by overcoming weakness

5. Trying to force happiness.

We can lift ourselves up and out of the traps that sabotage our happiness. We do not become happy by chance, we become happy by choice: true happiness is a lifestyle, not a moment by moment experience. It will require a change, and that change starts with attitude and a decision to be a happy person. Happiness is a better way to live and the mature success seeker creates priorities based on how it will affect his or her level of happiness. Acquiring anything that lacks value, significance, eternal purpose will eventually leave an internal void and diminish our happiness. Seek to be a happy person. Make decisions with a perspective of how happiness will be impacted. Let your disposition be one that portrays consistent love, joy, and a sound uplifting character and happiness will be a by product which unfolds success.

Sociologists, psychologist, clergy, and other leading human development professionals have determined that people who seek or have an anchor to a supreme power, a greater entity, a spiritual perspective, or a personal God are more likely to have a sense of great meaning and purpose in their lives — which in turn brings forth joy and happiness. Successful people know that a belief outside of yourself seems to enforce a feeling of assuredness which leads toward greater levels of experiencing success. People that have reached high levels of success have discovered that there is something about the supernatural that makes a difference for the better. The effect of an anchor to a higher being or God provides a signpost to guide a person in a course of life. It shows how to be a person of integrity, faithfulness, and care for others; how to have greater discipline, respect, and honor; and how to go to your personal God or your higher power when no one or nothing can help. Seekers of successful living know that our attitude and spiritual anchors play a part in creating an empowering life. And, really, this is the kind of life we desire most.

FIELD ACTIVITIES FROM YOUR SUCCESS COACH:

Take action of the following four items.

1. Make a list of four things that bring you happiness. What is it about these things that makes you happy?

2. Name four ways and four people you can share greater optimism:

3. Define your idea of a power greater than yourself. How is this an influence on your path of success?

4. Review and study the six virtues and the twenty four character traits. When, where and how can you implement them in your life?

5.2 The Beat Goes On

When faced with a mountain I will not quit!
I will keep on striving until I climb over, find a pass through,
tunnel underneath-
or simply stay and turn the mountain
into a gold mine, with God's help.

— ROBERT SCHULLER

During the 1960s a young songwriter named Sonny Bono used his intelligence and creativity to entertain America. He portrayed an image of a stoner, senseless, laughable hippy who played off the talents of his beautiful tall wife named Cher. Sonny wrote many songs, made a lot of money, and later became the mayor of one of the country's most desirable places to live, Palm Springs, California. His philosophy of life is that things happen and everyone will have difficulties, and troublesome events do occur. Don't let the challenges of life hold you back, keep on going. Thus comes one of the all-time classic hits. "The beat goes on."

At times it seems like the trials and transitions of our lives are constant and never-ending. It's like all I hope for is a season where I receive more pleasure than pain. Of course, we have all felt that way at some point. So, what do we do? Don't quit, keep moving, and don't give up. There are many factors that cause people to quit on their life purpose and goals. Fear is certainly in the top five percentile. Either fear of success or fear of failure is often the reason. In 1987, Susan Jeffers, PhD, wrote an insightful book called, *Feel the Fear and Do It Anyway.* In it she encourages her readers to connect to what's theirs, to give of themselves, to challenge themselves in spite of the fear. To be successful we must address our fears and move toward faith in the possibilities.

Another obstacle that holds people back and causes many to quit is not getting over the failures of the past. For many people, yesterday's losses and shoulda's often affect us and last a long time, which obviously affects our future. It keeps people living in the past and looking at life from the rearview mirror. This, of course, is not beneficial, especially for the success-driven person. The animated film, "The Lion King" gives us a pointed lesson on leaving the past and its failures in the past. The story centers on a young lion cub named Simba who was to be king but departed from his tribe because he mistakenly felt responsible for the death of his beloved father. The tribe falls apart in the absence of a great leader. Raffeeke, the tribe's wise medicine man, who is a baboon, seeks to counsel Simba to forget the past and come back to lead the tribe. Simba argues and sulks saying, "If I go back I must face the past and the pain." Raffeeke, while in disagreement, clobbers Simba over the head with a stick. Simba, startled, says, "Ouch, that hurt! What did you do that for?" Rafeeke responded, "What does it matter? It's in the past."

To constantly dwell on our past mistakes only perpetuates the issues. We all have a past, and some are more painful and filled with more failures than others. The success-minded person will come to terms with ineffective ways of viewing the past and can use what happened as a spring board for the future. See the past as a learning and growing experience. I once heard a teacher say to his student, "If I can't teach you from my examples, learn from my mistakes." All the mistakes and failures of the past can actually serve us. Many people are ill-advised about the fortunes that failure can bring us. They misunderstand, they fear it, and they run from it. The high rate of suicide, addictions, and other self-destructive behaviors often are the result of an inability to handle failure.

> "THE SUCCESS-MINDED PERSON WILL COME TO TERMS WITH INEFFECTIVE WAYS OF VIEWING THE PAST AND CAN USE WHAT HAPPENED AS A SPRING BOARD FOR THE FUTURE."

Failure can help us find our way toward success. Another way of looking at it is that you will more fully appreciate the success you have when you value the failures it took for you to have your success. Charles C. Manz, PhD, author of the book *The Power of Failure- 27 ways to turn life's setbacks into success* said,

> "Successful failure can become an important part of living a full and successful life. Every significant new venture, new skill

learned, or exciting opportunity pursued will bring with it the likelihood of experiencing short-term failure along the way. These setbacks can become important building blocks of success. Learn to be on the lookout for ways to use the power of failure everyday to live a more prosperous, productive, and peaceful life."

Ask any high achieving individual about the topic of failure and an honest response is often, "I know it well." More times than not, the only way to the mountain top is through the valley and in many cases, a series of valleys. Nancy, a friend and well respected teacher has had her share of highs and lows, wins and losses, gains and pains. She believes that her failures has been a benefit to her growth. She says, "Everything I've learned about success I've learned from my mistakes and failures. I wouldn't be the woman I am today and right now I wouldn't want it any other way." Many successful people have failed their way to success as if failure were a prerequisite to their success. When we change the energy and reframe our beliefs about failures, we begin to use failure to our advantage. Effective beliefs of success-minded people are:

Failure:

- happens to all of us but doesn't last forever.

- happens but it's your perception that matters.

- happens for greater learning and maturing.

- happens as a wake-up call to try something new.

Place yourself in the position to be a success regardless of the setbacks in your life. Make a declaration and be determined to succeed in spite of the accumulations of failures. I would much rather be under the instruction and mentorship of one who has failed and regrouped for success than on one who has not endured failure.

Consider this: It doesn't matter what you've done yesterday, it is gone. It doesn't matter where or how you've done it, it is not to appear again. It doesn't matter what mistakes happened or things you attempted and it didn't work out. What matters is your learning and that you don't quit.

Dreaming of starting a professional training school is easy, the real test is making it a reality. The Centre: a career training school was founded in 2001. www.newvibetraining.com. My first few years as founder and director seem to be positively moving toward growth. The third year was a true testing year for me. I found myself often discouraged and felt like closing shop until a trusted colleague shared a quote by the Philosopher Epititus. It read, "Adversity introduces a person to themselves." That quote spoke to me. I soon saw that difficult time as a teaching season just for me. It taught me many lessons, but particularly about myself. How to manage business adversity, how to let go, how to overcome, and not give up when times are tough.

We celebrated our tenth anniversary and we keep growing as a professional training school where thousands of students have transformed their lives through our teaching and coaching. We now teach at several Universities and Community Colleges. It would not have happened if I had quit because it was tough.

Actor Clint Eastwood in the movie, *Heartbreak Ridge* used a phrase for overcoming obstacles: "Improvise, adapt, and overcome." That's what we must repeatedly think and say to ourselves when we feel like we want to falter.

People who know success have learned valuable lessons from obstacles and failures:

- They learn to wake up the next morning and try again.

- They learn to manage their disappointments

- They learn how to wait and sometimes wait a while.

Make the effort to get up, dust yourself off, make adjustments, and keep going. Resilience is an important ingredient to the success formula. You never know what life path could be transformed or whose very life could be saved because you didn't quit, you kept your goal alive, you improvised, you adapted, and you overcame.

As a kid growing up in the Pacific Northwest, Tim Leatherman loved the outdoors. His father, a carpenter, shared fishing, camping, and a curiosity toward fixing things. Tim eventually left for college and graduated with a Mechanical Engineering degree. After college young people usually seek two things: a job and a partner. Tim found both. The job was not satisfying, but the partner was and he soon married. He and his bride spent time traveling overseas and on one occasion he traveled all the way to Asia, a journey he used to reflect on his purpose. He called it their "what are we going to do with the rest of our lives?" trip.

Tim was a handyman with a keen mind. He was often inclined to take out his pocket boy scout knife to fix broken items as he traveled. On this Asian trip he landed on an idea, and that was to create a pair of pliers in a pocket knife. He was determined to take only seven days to develop the prototype and secure a patent in place, instead it took him three years. Finally after many attempts he designed and produced a finished product, which is now known as the popular Leatherman tool.

He encountered challenges from the beginning. Initially he couldn't find a venue to sell his product or a willing customer to take a risk on something new. He approached the telephone company, the U.S. Army, and others. He was turned down everywhere. Some said that this was not a knife, but a tool. Some said this was not a tool, but a gadget. It took eight more years until, finally, a mail order catalogue decided to purchase just a small order.

Tim was discouraged after such a huge emotional investment, time investment, and money investment. He was ready to give up when suddenly he started receiving calls for more orders from other mail order catalogues. Soon his product was in demand, and within a year after that order he sold over 70,000 tools. The company today has over 350 employees with over two and a half million Leatherman tools sold yearly. Tim improvised, he adapted, and he overcame. He did not quit. I asked Tim Leatherman how he believed he has contributed to the world because of his persistence to not give up. In reply he faxed me the following news article from The Anchorage Daily News from January 28, 1992.

Broken down at 12,000 Ft, Try Anything

As his plane climbed toward the Alaska Range, Manokotak Air pilot Mike Harder was upside down, under the instrument panel, using his "Leatherman" pocket tool trying to repair landing gear that wouldn't come down. For the better part of an hour he struggled to make midair repairs, while his co-pilot flew, talked to mechanics over the radio and made arrangements for a crash landing. Harder, the airline's owner and chief pilot, and his co-pilot were bringing the Piper Navajo twin-engine craft to Dillingham January 8 when the landing gear bound up. The emergency backup system also failed. "We had two choices," Harder said. "Crash in Dillingham (or return to Anchorage International Airport) and crash in Anchorage." But stiff head winds made it impossible to reach Anchorage before running out of fuel. Harder decided to find the problem himself, consulting with mechanics on the ground. He got out his Leatherman tool, a compact folding set of pliers, screwdrivers, knife blade, file, can opener and other tools. It was a recent gift from a friend, and the only tool on board. He opened up the instrument panel from below, dug around a little and finally found a broken cable. "I was able to get one strand of cable with the pliers," Harder said. "I pulled it slowly and four more strands came out." He kept pulling and with a "clunk, clunk, clunk," the gear descended and locked. The pair landed in Dillingham. "They called it a day, and took the next day off," said chief mechanic Jim McMurray.

— Malcolm Wright
Bristol Bay Times and Dutch Harbor Fisherman

If Tim Leatherman would have gathered his tools and gone home, given up on his goal, or just quit, quite possibly Harder and his co-pilot would not have made it to their destination alive. Tim Leatherman had a contribution to make to this world. He helped in his own way to keep life alive and somehow make good on that contribution thousands of miles away. We must be persistent and seek ways to bounce back from failure. For the success seeker the lesson here is never stop believing in what is true for you, never give up, never let the past postpone your possibilities, never let your failures determine your future. Never ever quit in life. You will be challenged but for success to become a reality you must keep the beat going on.

FIELD ACTIVITIES FROM YOUR SUCCESS COACH:

Take action on these two items.

1. **Assess a recent failure using the following questions:**

   - What was the situation?

   - Was what happened a true failure?

   - How did it fall short of desired outcome?

   - What success came from this?

   - What is my learning?

   - How am I grateful?

   - What do I need now?

   - Where do I go from here?

   - How do I help others succeed from failure?

2. **What affirmation, declaration, quote, or saying would be helpful for you to memorize and repeat when the going gets challenging. Record it on a 3x5 card. Review as a reminder.**

5.3 Working on a Goals Mind

*Give me a stock clerk with a goal and I'll give you
a man who will make history.
But give me a man without a goal and I'll give you
a stock clerk.*

— JC PENNEY FOUNDER

It certainly doesn't have to be this way, but the reality is that many people live their lives with little, if any, direction. It seems each developmental life stage is experienced aimlessly, unmapped, and uncharted. After a period of time, these individuals have lost any and all motivation for success, mostly because of a continuous unplanned lifestyle.

People who are determined to have success find that goals strongly affects the course of events. Those who are serious about success find the importance of goals and make them a priority. They are go getters, goal setters, and gold sustainers. They succeed primarily because they set up a course for themselves so they know where they are going — and they take action for accomplishments. Setting goals is the most basic step toward achieving anything worthwhile. It is also a must if you are seeking to be purposeful in deciding how you are going to live. What if you were sitting in the airplane ready for take off when suddenly you heard the pilot say, "Welcome aboard people, this is your Captain speaking. We will be taking off at some point and we will fly in a random direction and eventually land in an area somewhere off in the distance..." I'm sure your response would be, "Get me outta here!!" Just like pilots who know their goals, and set out for their destination through careful planning, navigating, and adjusting to stay the course, so must you if you are serious about success.

If you are a person who wants to achieve, then the master skill to obtain is the ability to slow down, concentrate, and set goals personally and professionally. The things that will transform you from where you are today to where you want to be tomorrow are the books you read, the people you associate with, and the goals you set and reach. A life devoid of specific goals to move toward is mediocre at best. All success-centered people are oriented toward a mindset of setting goals and believing they will achieve them. Goals are powerful and a must for health, wealth, and living a life of purpose and prosperity.

> "THE THINGS THAT WILL TRANSFORM YOU FROM WHERE YOU ARE TODAY TO WHERE YOU WANT TO BE TOMORROW ARE THE BOOKS YOU READ, THE PEOPLE YOU ASSOCIATE WITH, AND THE GOALS YOU SET AND REACH."

Jack Welch, one of history's most accomplished CEOs, accepted the leadership role at General Electric and endorsed goals to transform the culture. At 45, he was a maverick at how to create and perform the largest corporate makeover. He started by believing in what can be possible through the people that came to work daily and the goals they set for achievement. Welch felt there was no limit to what people can do when there was a target to aim at. He had a favorite saying, "There is unlimited juice in the lemon." He believed people in organizations can reach the stars when they stretch themselves to accomplish professional and personal goals.

Goals are an important part of our life and the intentions behind goals are also important. Even the thief has a goal. Beware of seeking goals based on envy, retaliation, or hurtful motives. Instead, focus your intention to learn the strategies of accomplishing meaningful, purposeful, and quality goals. The things we want to accomplish certainly will not happen by accident. The true purpose of setting and achieving goals is what it will make of you as a person, the quality of character that will be produced. Goals begin early in life. Studies indicate that early childhood development formulates lifelong thinking patterns toward setting goals. A child will have a natural tendency to move toward or repeat behavior that brings positive feelings or outcomes. What we love and do well as children will result in talents as adults.

Psychologists tracked fifty people beginning at age seven and reevaluated them every seven years until age 35. Surprisingly, all subjects found work that was related to interests they had demonstrated between the ages of seven and fourteen. Although most of them had discarded or strayed from those interests in early adulthood, virtually all had found their way back to their childhood aspirations by age 35.

I remember training for my first triathlon. My first practice I swam the length of the pool and thought to myself, "could I be way over my head in accomplishing this goal?" I decided to take small steps and monitor my progress weekly. After four months of setting and achieving small goals, I completed a one mile swim, a 30 mile bike ride and a 6 mile run. My first triathlon was a personal success. It happened because I commited myself to setting and reaching specific goals.

The beginning process of achieving goals is to first set them. According to Webster's Dictionary "to set" means to put or fix in a direction; to start out on a course; to become lodged, to place oneself in a position of action. Let's translate that into sitting down and in a journal or note-pad write out an outline, create a plan, and then follow it. It is true: if you fail to plan, you plan to fail. Goals can only be achieved through a clear, specific, and precise plan — a plan that you must whole- heartedly and 100% believe in, a plan that you must relentlessly take action upon, a plan that will passionately motivate you. In order to get what you set out to obtain, you must thoughtfully execute your plan. Implement the eight elements of a goal and use the SMARRT model to outline the strategic steps of your plan.

Eight Elements of a Goal:

The first element, a goal must be something that can and must be **achievable.**

- Is it realistic and attainable? Visualize achieving the goal. Believe you can do it. Reaching for a goal enlarges your faith. Use action verbs to describe what needs to be done. Some examples: reduce, increase, develop, create, eliminate, etc.

- Clarify what you want to do with positive emotions. Clarification is usually highlighted by your action verb choice.

The second element of a goal is that a goal must be **regulated.**

- It answers the question: "How will I know when I've accomplished what I set out to do?"

- It provides the signposts you can use to assess, gauge, and evaluate your progress.

- It sets measurements that you can understand and are willing to use for information.

The third element of a goal is that it contains a time element, some reference to a specific point in **time.**

- "What specific step or time do I take action?" "When do I need to do the tasks?"

- "What stages of timeline" and "What is the deadline?"

The fourth element of a goal is a **cost** consideration.

- "How much money am I willing to commit to achieve this goal?"

- "How many other resources am I willing to commit to achieve this goal?"

The fifth element of a goal is **writing** your goals down.

- You must consistently write your goals down. Unwritten goals are just daydreams. They must be written down to become concrete.

- Continually writing and checking off your goals significantly increases your chance of success.

The sixth element of a goal is that it is **read** regularly, frequently, and with emotion.

- The most successful people refer to their goals on a daily basis. It helps keep your energy up and your mind alert.

- Reading them consistently helps you maintain your focus and stay motivated to achieve. You cannot remember what you cannot see.

The seventh element of a goal takes into account influential **relationships.**

- What impact will working toward this goal have on you? Your family? Your colleagues? Other people?

- What are the overall effects when you achieve your goal? Be mindful. Goal attainment may change your beliefs, routines, habits, associations, etc.

The eighth element of a goal considers the **effects** of the goal achieved.

- Goal attainment requires intention and motivation. Are you willing to commit the energy, time, money to achieving your goal?

- How dedicated are you? What adjustments will you make? What are you committed to and willing to not give up?

The SMARRT Model:

The S.M.A.R.R.T system will help you put goals into action.

S.M.A.R.R.T stands for:

S: **Specific.** Goals must be specific and well defined.

M: **Measurable.** Goals must be measurable.

A: **Action.** Goals will be accomplished only when action is taken.

R   **Realistic.** Goals must be realistic and attainable.

R: **Resources.** Goals must assess money, energy, associates, etc.

T: **Time.** Goals must have a strong consideration of time elements.

Successful people know that the journey of goals begins with knowing who you are and aligning with your values. From who you are is revealed what is important to you; what is important to you reveals your goals. Experienced goal setters have a working system and live on paper. They take small manageable steps and progress strategically. They write out on paper daily, weekly, monthly goals. They have a ledger, journal, or goal-setting notepad with their quarterly goals, twelve month goals, three year goals, five year goals, and ten year goals.

The list of goals to work on often comes from the eight components of a life balance wheel. There are various types of life balance listings. These are the specific ones I use, which are listed in this format: 1. mental, 2. emotional, 3. financial, 4. life work, 5. social, 6. health, 7. relationship, and 8. spiritual. Within each balance component create levels of assessments. Create a scale from 1 to 10. Draw a line and mark on the left end 0 and on the right end a 10, find the middle and mark a 5. Do a self evaluation on your life in each balance component. Assess…If you are low, develop a plan and set goals to get higher. We can have a great life and be successful. Fall in love with Goal setting. Start with your daily goals, today.

Life Balance Wheel

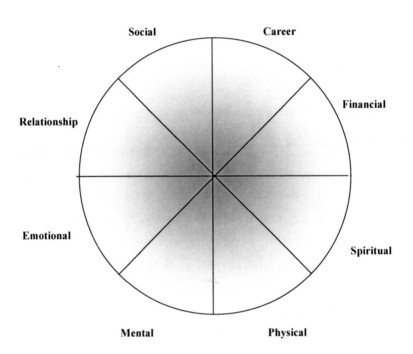

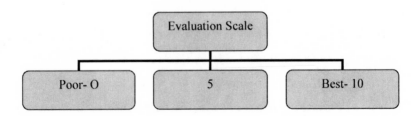

FIELD ACTIVITIES FROM YOUR SUCCESS COACH:

Take action for greater balance in life.

1. From the Life Balance Wheel determine what four areas of your life are in greater balance. List in order of highest to lowest. List the four areas of least balance in order. Observe what's working in the high level of balance. Determine through goal setting how to bring each area of the least balance to a higher balance.

2. Identify two people. Be it friend, associate, mentor or a professional that can assist you to reach your goals. Start with showing them your outline of your life in balance and out of balance.

Chapter Five

SIX VIP'S for Success Seekers

Successful people know that:

1. Success has a formula to follow. It involves being a go getter, goal setter, and gold maintainer.

2. Success begins and ends with an attitude that is positive, passionate, and productive.

3. Success is forever evolving. As long as we live, we never stop seeking success.

4. Success has transformational power. It brings forth poise and deep character illumination.

5. Success happens with action in full motion. Outcomes are obtained by consciously and strategically going after what you want.

6. Success unfolds through the lessons we learn when we fail and with a relentless mindset of never quitting.

Chapter Six
Step 6: Advance Forward to Your Destination

NOTHING IN LIFE IS WORTH MORE THAN WHERE YOU ARE TODAY. BE A LIFELONG LEARNER. CELEBRATE ALL THAT LIVING HAS TO OFFER AND ADVANCE TO YOUR DESTINY OF LIVING SUCCESSFULLY.

Successful people know that people want to be involved with things that are successful and built to last. It's about the total quality of success, not just the quantity. It must be solid as a rock because quality of success is noticeable, desirable, and contagious and can do wonders for everyone. It makes a person go one of two ways. It either makes a person a prima donna with their poor development of personality, or it can produce attractive character traits that everyone admires and seeks after. For those who take full advantage of the life changing qualities success offers, it brings full value. It happens with the accumulation of many small positive efforts in the flow of moving forward toward your destiny of living successfully.

To maximize your success requires a consistency of disciplined thinking and a consistency of disciplined behavior over a period of time. Nothing is automatic; it's developmental. With the attitude of seeking excellence, with the attainment of success there will be a following of people who respect you because of how you responded to your growth and good fortune. It's a positive model for others. Success is a good thing for everyone, so it's important to share. It's revolutionizing and about creating abundance for the greater good. To do that you must take care of your business in order to add something great to your life and this world. It doesn't matter if it's starting an entrepreneurial venture to help employ people. It doesn't matter if it is raising a healthy child, starting a non-profit, or climbing the highest peak on a mountain. The business of a successful person is to personally take care of your life and your surroundings and to keep the momentum going with determination to keep building for the future. To add a benefit to everything you attract, no matter what or who it is.

Andre Agassi, now a retired professional athlete was one of only five men in history to win each of the four Grand Slam Tournaments in tennis. He was interviewed by Parade magazine (2007) on life after tennis. He stated, "There are a lot of life lessons that you learn through tennis. One big lesson: always look forward. Once a game or set is done you focus on what's next." Retired at 37 years old, he currently is writing his memoir, designing a high end furniture line, developing a series of real estate projects and busy being a father and a husband. In addition, one of his favorite endeavors was establishing the Andre Agassi College Academy for disadvantage youth, which was honored as a national model charter school. It graduated it's first class in 2009. Andre says, "There is just so much more. I feel like it's a canvas, and I don't want to paint it all at once." Successful people keep creating, they ask the question: What's next?

George Bernard Shaw the successful playwright and famous literary personality of the 20th century was a self proclaimed writing machine.

A popular piece of work was *Pygmalion*, later adapted into a Broadway musical called, "My Fair Lady." He remained active with a mindset of what's next until his death at 94 years old. He once said "I dread success. To have succeeded is to have finished one's business on earth, like the male spider that is killed by the female the moment he has succeeded in his courtship. I like a state of continual becoming, with a goal in front and not behind." Keep asking: What is next? Keep moving forward everyday. We cannot rest on our laurels. Success must keep on rolling. We cannot look to be secure, for there is no security. There is only opportunity and possibilities; therefore you must make the best of success and keep progress advancing forward because truly you are getting better everyday.

> "WE CANNOT LOOK TO BE SECURE, FOR THERE IS NO SECURITY. THERE IS ONLY OPPORTUNITY AND POSSIBILITIES; THEREFORE YOU MUST MAKE THE BEST OF SUCCESS AND KEEP ADVANCING FORWARD BECAUSE TRULY YOU ARE GETTING BETTER EVERYDAY."

6.1 Taking Care of Business Everyday

A person on the path of success recognizes that much of the cares of our daily life is about taking good care of business; the business of your life everyday. It could be personal business or professional business, but if you reflect deeply enough you'll discover every aspect of our lives involves some kind of business that we must care for. For our business of living to exhibit dramatic movement upward we must really care, we must be attentive, we must wholeheartedly contribute what is needed everyday. The well known motivational and empowerment author and speaker, Mr. Jim Rohn said, "Success is nothing more than a few simple disciplines practiced everyday."

If you are seeking to achieve you must establish positive routines and daily habits of taking special care of the business of your individual path toward success. Believe me, if you are determined and serious about success, there will be plenty to take care of. Begin with getting in the business of taking care of yourself, because you are all you've got. You must be able to function well in order to get maximum potential out of you. This life is not a dress rehearsal and everything you do or don't do has an influence toward an end result. When you consider how important it is to be a loving partner, to be a responsible parent, to be a good citizen, to be a loyal employee, or a competent employer, it is essential to invest in you in order to be your best and get the best.

I am always in a state of wonderment at those individuals who are reluctant to invest in themselves. We want to establish success that is equipped for more success and built for the endurance of life. There is a distinct difference from those who invest in themselves and those who do not. What you do for yourself counts, so take care of yourself. There are those who believe self-care was reserved for the rich and famous, and the so-called "normal folks" would have to be satisfied with an occasional splurge. Not true! A myth! A faulty belief!

As you nurture and take care of your personal self you will attract opportunities. You attract opportunities because your standards are higher and your level of effectiveness brings forth abundant results. For the success minded individual, it is paramount that you commit to taking care of you and your duties of living well everyday. It must be repeated, it must have long exposure, and it must finally become an ingrained habit. Aristotle said, "We are what we repeatedly do; excellence then, is not an act, but a habit." I often hear from well accomplished individuals that their success came when they formed habits that supported their outcome. It was something that took place everyday of their lives. Whether it is taking your vitamins, reading the sports page, being loving, making your bed, saying your prayers, exercising, whatever it is.

A memorable experience I had in connection with the importance of taking care of the business of your life everyday came in 1987 when I was introduced to a 73 year old person I highly admired. This person left a lasting influence on me to this day. He once invited me to a front row seat at his seminar. You can just imagine my elation. His message was centered on his journey of success which required daily attention. He came from a poor family during the depression, a sickly, depressed, angry fifteen year old youth who failed at suicide several times. He once tried to set his home on fire and attempted to attack his older brother with a butcher knife. He suffered greatly from migraines with no relief in sight. There was little known about remedies to cure his discomfort, no anti-depressants or prescription medicine. He was instructed by a doctor to experiment with moving to warmer weather or possibly wetter weather. He took action on the recommendation and nothing worked until he was invited to a health lecture by a pioneer nutritionist named Paul Bragg.

In his presentation, Mr. Bragg spoke about eating and exercise, and the benefits of eliminating sugars and harmful drinks and foods from our diets. A lifestyle this young man was not familiar with. He began to eat fruits, vegetables, whole grains, took supplements, and exercised everyday. He dedicated himself to learning more and was able to create and sustain healthy habits to empower his life. He greatly improved his health and entire well-being and soon created a fitness enterprise. In 1936, he opened the nation's first modern health studio which changed his life and millions of other lives forever. His name is Jack Lalanne, and he is the father of a revolution in fitness, health and wellness.

He was heavily criticized by the medical field, but his methods were tested and proven to be sound as he developed the first prototype of exercise equipment. Although he himself confesses that he hates to exercise, he knows it produces what he wants, living a successful life. Because of his daily commitment to be successful, he accomplished some of the following incredible feats.

- At age 40 in 1954 he set an undisputed world record by swimming the length of the San Francisco Golden Gate Bridge underwater with 140 pounds of equipment. That's unbelievable!

- At age 43, he set a world record of 1,033 push-ups in 23 minutes. That's unheard of!

- At age 45, he completed 1,000 push-ups and 1,000 chin-ups in 1 hour and 22 minutes and the Jack LaLanne Show goes nationwide. That's insane!

- At age 60, he swam from Alcatraz Island to Fisherman's Wharf, for a second time handcuffed, shackled and towing a 1,000 pound boat; and gatorade had been around less than nine yers. That's over the top!

- At age 62, commemorating the "Spirit of 76", swam 1 mile in Long Beach Harbor, handcuffed, shackled, and towing 13 boats (representing the 13 original colonies) containing 76 people. That's unforgettable!

- At age 70 and handcuffed, shackled, and fighting strong winds and currents, he towed 70 boats with 70 people from the Queen's Way Bridge in the Long Beach Harbor to the Queen Mary for 1 1/2 miles. That's phenomenal!

- In 1994 at age 80, he received the Governor's Council on Physical Fitness Lifetime Achievement Award from the state of California. Eight years later he received his own star on the Hollywood Boulevard Walk of Fame. That's memorable!

- In 2004 at age 90, he celebrates his birthday with a supersize media blitz in New York, San Francisco, and Los Angeles. ESPN Classic runs a 24 -hour marathon of the original Jack LaLanne TV Shows. That's a tribute!

These accomplishments are amazing. It happened with a strong and consistent daily routine. In 2010, Jack LaLanne left this earth. Jack and his wife Elaine were enthusiastic entrepreneurs who had published several books, and created various health and wellness products. Jack continued to move forward in creating a quality of living for greater success well into his last days. His motivational message has swept the country for generations and the outcomes have been beneficial to millions. Day after day for many years, they took care of business and they loved it. The effective effort you put out everyday has a boomerang effect: it comes back to you. Your investment is never wasted. Just make the investment and more possibilities for greater success will be added to your life.

Successful people know that seeds of success must be planted everyday. Weeds will grow if you're not careful, not attentive, and not present. One must be and stay honest, humble, and hungry for the harvest of success will appear; have faith, create, and build everyday. There is truth to the saying, "If you build it, they will come" from the 1998 movie *Field of Dreams*. When people sense success they are:

- Energized

- Self assured

- Visualizing positive outcomes

- Communicating enthusiastically

- In action

- Mindful

- Coachable

When people sense failure they:

- Look for excuses

- Are negative

- Lose energy

- Settle

- Give up

- Not coachable

Plant the seeds of development and growth every day and your life will surely take root and sprout for living abundantly.

Taking care of business everyday requires endurance. Think of the marathon runners who train themselves for the race. Their motivation is to build up and have strong endurance. Nobody wakes up on the morning of the New York Marathon and suddenly decides to join the race. The marathon runner spends months in preparation. Then when the race arrives, throughout the 26.2 miles their body goes through changes; finding the right pace, overcoming exhaustion, possible muscle cramps, and the sometimes whispering negative inner voice midway through the race that can hamper the runner's confidence. To get to this race requires proper eating, sleeping, thinking, and training every day. This endurance is designed to have staying power and initiative to do what it takes to keep stepping forward and stay in the race. This is what gets you to the goal line. To be a success it will require you to be in daily contact with your passion and purpose and run the race everyday.

FIELD ACTIVITIES FROM YOUR SUCCESS COACH:

Taking action will increase your daily effectiveness. Recommend these three exercises.

1. **How can you exercise your intention for success everyday? Write at the beginning of your journal page, "My intention for success today is:" Using the balance wheel, clearly write out your intentions to be successful in the component of your life. Write everyday.**

2. **Follow the Ten Everyday Tips for Steady Success:**

    1. Every day, breathe, breathe, breathe. Start your day with deep breathing exercise. It will circulate the blood flow, help you be clear in your thinking, and aid your body to combat anxiety and stress.

    2. Every day, identify what is causing tension and be assertive to find a solution. Life is short, so be aware and identify what is the cause of your pain. Be pro-active.

3. Every day, allow time for yourself. Take time to create in your schedule a routine of being alone, to be still, to reflect, to meditate, to pray, to be with moments that nurture you.

4. Every day, engage in wisdom reading (preferably in the morning). Read motivational, devotional, or inspirational material daily to program your brain in the direction that guides the best in you.

5. Every day, give and receive love. Love is exciting. Find simple ways to share love and to receive it. Also, get the appropriate amounts of rest and nutrition. A well-balanced life is plenty of rest, good food and a lot of love.

6. Every day, rid yourself of dysfunction, including relationships that hurt. Set clear limits with people who control, who manipulate, and who are hurtful. Our language is an indicator of what's in the heart.

7. Every day, bring passionate meaning to your vocation. Let your work be a place where you enjoy going to because you love what you do.

8. Every day, share kindness as well as laughter. Find joy in being kind toward everyone you meet. Share something fun; it's worth a good laugh.

9. Every day, learn something new to improve yourself in your personal and professional world. Be a life-long learner to improve your life. You will feel good about what you have accomplished.

10. Every day, commit to live the way you wish to be remembered. Have you decided what you want others to think of you when you are gone? In the movie "Gladiator" Maximus announces, "What we do in life echoes in eternity." Start today to leave a legacy of a good character and successful person.

3. How can you place specific areas of your personal life into a business mentally? How will this make a difference?

6.2 I'd Like to Teach the World to Succeed

Liberty cannot be preserved without a general knowledge among the people....
Let us dare to read, think, speak and write.

— JOHN ADAMS

One of my favorite songs is by Louis Armstrong called, "What a Wonderful World." Whenever I hear it, I just want to soak it up. It makes me want to share the meaning with others. It really is about all the things that are successful about our world. For those in pursuit of success, one of the most rewarding things is to teach others to be successful. Success-minded individuals know that they acquired their success because they dedicated themselves to learn how to be a success. Any significant improvement in our lives can be attributed to how much was delivered to us by teaching and how much we desired to learn.

Our learning is a major factor in how success will influence our lives. In our ever-changing society, education has taken on a greater role. In fact, our workplace culture has gone from an industrial age to an information age. It is not just about what is being taught or the educational program; it is the ability to have the skill of learning that matters most. Many believe education is specifically for the young. It seems the objective is to go to formal schooling to complete a higher degree or degrees status in order to get a job and earn a good living. However, at its core education and learning do form a total sense of integration. Once a person commits to being a learner, they simultaneously become an integral part of their own educational program.

Thomas Edison, an inventor and businessman known for inventions like the phonograph, the light bulb, and the first industrial research laboratory, had only three months of formal education. Because of his wandering ways and short attention span, he was sent home, to be home-schooled by his mother. Without formal schooling he still demonstrated strong commitment and desire to pursue learning which impacted the world. Other well-known inventors and entrepreneurs like Henry Ford, the Wright brothers, and Sam Walton had little, if any, formal education but they had the quality of being self-directed learners whose personal inquiry empowered their activities and subject matter. Learning is constantly happening. We must be mindful of how it is present and impacting our lives for greater success. Jay Rifenbarg, author of the book *No Excuse*, wrote, "The catalyst for true success is learning."

Personal learning is unparalleled. We are all learning in a different way as we are different in our learning from everyone else. We cannot escape — learning is all around us. We all grow, develop, and mature in our learning as we experience life and as we live day by day. In the late 17th century, John Locke, considered one of the most influential philosophers of post-renaissance Europe and called the father of human psychology, wrote and delivered an essay that was based on the model of how humans develop, form ideas, learn, and unfold their personalities. His theory was the *tabula rosa,* a Latin phrase meaning "blank slate." Locke's theory is that we are born with a blank slate and it is our daily intake of learning that expands us. Daily life continually shapes our minds and matures our personalities. This was a great leap for other great thinkers to probe the understanding of learning and personality types. Two hundred years later Dr. Carl Jung, a psychologist, explored further concepts of learning and personality types which influenced Isabel Myer and her mother Katherine Briggs to develop a learning and personality assessment called the Myer Briggs Type Indicator (MBTI), used widely by various professionals in the helping field. We are all learners, and success-oriented people use the value of learning as a catalyst for success.

In the book, *Peak Learning,* author Ronald Gross creates an answer to the question of "what is learning" using Robert M Smith's description. "Learning is basically an activity of one who learns. It may be intentional or random; it may involve acquiring new information or skills, new attitudes, understandings or values. It usually is accompanied by change in behavior and goes on throughout life. It is often thought of as both process and outcome. Education can be defined as the organized systematic effort to foster learning, to establish the conditions, and to provide the activities through which learning can occur." To involve learning to a greater and more powerful degree recognizes that our brain has two hemispheres and both have distinctive areas of strengths. The left side of the brain has greater analytical focus, while the right side has more creative focus. Learn to use and exercise both sides with activities that utilize our full bran and learning capacity.

Dolly Rebecca Parton is a person whose voice, talent, and image are instantly recognizable in the U.S and around the globe. A singer, songwriter, and an entrepreneur, she has sold over 100 million records worldwide, has won seven Grammies, nine Country Music Association awards, and has been named a living legend by the Library of Congress. Dolly grew up poor in a Tennessee mountain cabin with ten other siblings. She was committed to learning at an early age. She wrote her first song at five years old, and at ten years old she was traveling to Knoxville to appear on a local television variety show. Dolly gives credit to her family who encouraged her to pursue her own life dreams and from her own innate desire to learn and keep on learning.

She also has a passion for spreading the importance of learning. In her autobiography, *Dolly: My Life and Other Unfinished Business,* Parton discloses her love for learning, including reading everything she could get her hands on from the Bible to the Farmers Almanac. But she also had to work at learning. She said, "Believe me, I was not the best student in the world, but I loved books, magazines, and catalogues. When I was growing up, we didn't have a television and rarely went to the movies, so reading was the only way to know about a world outside of the Smoky Mountains. Once I knew about the world, I wanted to get there as soon as possible."

In 1996 she founded the Imagination Library. Its purpose was to provide a new book every month to children from birth to age five. Now in operation in 42 states and 4 Canadian provinces, the Imagination Library Foundation and its local sponsoring organization serve 330,000 children and distribute close to 4 million books a year. The first book each child receives is *The Little Engine that Could,* a classic that tells the story of a determined little train that overcomes doubters and obstacles to make it over the mountain. The mission for her foundation: help kids dream more, learn more, care more, and be more. Instilling the passion of learning at an early age opens the door to success in the later years.

During an earlier time in my life one of the greatest pleasures I experienced was to be able to read to two precious little people who opened their hearts to learn, six-year-old Gabriel and three-year-old Emelia Rose. They could not wait for their bedtime story. They listened enthusiastically, grasping the meaning of the message. Learning was a happy time for these wonderful children. Gabriel would always check to see if he had his favorite book under his pillow before he said goodnight; it was a white children's Bible with colorful pictures. Emelia Rose would sweetly say what she was grateful for today. The joy of learning and the life benefits to these beautiful little children will influence their future ability to succeed in a great and mighty way. Take note: it's never too late. This holds true for adult learners as well. Success-minded people teach others to learn because it's from our learning that brings forth success.

> "THEY COULD NOT WAIT FOR THEIR BEDTIME STORY. THEY LISTENED ENTHUSIASTICALLY, GRASPING THE MEANING OF THE MESSAGE. LEARNING WAS A HAPPY TIME FOR THESE WONDERFUL CHILDREN."

Education and learning is serious business in Kalamazoo, Michigan. On November 10, 2005, Janice M. Brown, the superintendent of the Kalamazoo Public Schools, enthusiastically stepped up to announce something that had never been announced in this nation. That was that all students who would be graduating with a 2.0 or better, who resided in the district, and had been a student for four or more years, got their entire post-secondary education, college tuition, including fees, completely paid for at a public university or community college in the State of Michigan. This is called the Kalamazoo Promise. It was the brainstorming idea of a small group of anonymous donors from the community who had regularly met for three years to discuss ways to keep students in school, help the economy, attract new business development, and add to the quality of life to Western Michigan — particularly the city of Kalamazoo. Over 12 million dollars in scholarship funds is available for students who have a desire to be their best by way of learning. The first class to receive this promise was the 2006 class in which 500 students graduated. 400 students were eligible for the full scholarship, 375 have applied, and 335 have completed two full semesters. Wow! What a promise, what a gift! Invest in learning and education to bring forth greater success for everyone's benefit. With more promises like that, I can't help but think to myself, what a wonderful world! Believe in the promise — it works.

There are people who have answered their life calling to inspire success through education and learning. Oprah Winfrey, one of the most beloved and influential woman in this world is one of them. To the delight of my loving mother, Daisy, Oprah has single handedly placed the benefits of success through learning and education in full view so the world at large can notice. Not only has Oprah created her own book club (called The Oprah Winfrey Book Club), started her own magazine "O". She pledged to make education a priority around the world. She has established a 501(c)3 organization called The Angel Network. So far, 60 new schools in 13 countries have been established. The most noticeable is The Oprah Winfrey Leadership Academy for Girls; lavishly built 40 miles SW of Johannesburg in South Africa. She pledged ten million dollars for the school and brought together 152 of the most inspirational girls to educate them and to help them be future leaders in this country.

Oprah was born into poverty in Mississippi and raised until the age of six by her grandmother who influenced the foundation for Oprah's success. She taught her early how to read and created a love of learning even before most children were learning how to talk. Books became her outlet. She grew up a voracious reader, a dedicated habit that she retains to this day. She stated, "My own love for learning and education was the reason for my success." She is the first African American woman to become a billionaire. Oprah's love and passion for learning was a model for many and for years she sat with over 20 million viewers everyday sharing, educating, and enhancing the message of success through learning. I believe if you were to ask Oprah if she was a fan of Louis Armstrong and took to heart his song "What a Wonderful World" you may have to sit down, relax, and listen as she possibly will serenade you. She might start by singing, "And I say to myself, 'What a wonderful world!'"

FIELD ACTIVITIES FROM YOUR SUCCESS COACH:

Take action on these three items.

1. **Start with a goal to read one book a month**. Write out what was learned in your reading. Motivate yourself to have a library in your home.

2. **Seek to enroll in one professional or personal development class within the next 14 days.**

3. **Volunteer in an educational setting to help children learn to read.** Try S.M.A.R.T. Start making a reader today.

6.3 Celebrate

"The best use people can make of their day is to enjoy it.
Then spread that joy unto others.
Celebrate your days while you have them."

— CARL CASANOVA

Life is moving at a rapid pace. As quick as a wink, you're now Senior Partner at the firm, your kids have their kids, and the marriage golden anniversary has arrived. It's a known fact that life comes at you fast, and for many there are thoughts like, "If I could just rewind the clock I would have had more fun, more laughter, and more moments to celebrate life…" More and more success seekers are including the art of celebration because they know NOW is the time to celebrate life, while you have life to celebrate.

What comes to mind when you think of celebrating? Does it conjure up expressions and images of festivity, dancing, eating, sharing, rejoicing, delighting, admiring, exalting, approving, and praising? Does the mire fact of reading these descriptions cause excitement within you? Does it remind you of possibly what's missing in your own life? Celebration and success go hand in hand, because success is cause for celebration; and the greater the frequency of celebration, the greater success you attract.

Life does not have to be perfect for celebration. Even the smallest wins or a special moment can and should be cause for celebration. I remember a time in my life when my constant drive toward accomplishment brought me to a state of frustration and irritation about the simplest things. I found myself distant from others and out of balance in my life. I couldn't put my finger on the remedy. Then a caring friend said, "Carl, stop and celebrate. Go and just smell the roses." At first I thought, "Who's got time to stop and, above all, smell roses? How ridiculous!?" Then I discovered that that was exactly what I needed to do — and I did it. I had no idea how that simple act would lower my anxiety and give me a new perspective. I soon realized how celebration is an integral part of living a life that is a success.

> "CELEBRATION AND SUCCESS GO HAND IN HAND BECAUSE SUCCESS IS CAUSE FOR CELEBRATION; AND THE GREATER THE FREQUENCY OF CELEBRATION, THE GREATER SUCCESS YOU ATTRACT."

The Law of Celebration states that there are ample reasons to celebrate life. Look for the beauty and share the joy. I heard the average human heart beats 100,000 times a day. Why not make each beat meaningful, expressive, and gratifying. Cultivating an attitude and mindset of celebration is making a statement about yourself. It says, "I will recognize the blessings." It says, "I will share abundance." For many, the spirit of celebration has been dampened, possibly by the cares and concerns of life's difficulties, possibly from childhood where celebration was never encouraged; or possibly from not having expanded their creativity or motivation to express celebration. An important life lesson I've personally discovered is that without celebration, success is hollow.

Whatever the reason, it's important to have celebration as an important value. If nothing else, it has health and wellness benefits associated with it. You can celebrate anything you like about your life at any time. Consider this: anytime you accomplish a goal, celebrate. Anytime you are connected with family or friends, celebrate. Anytime you find a solution to a challenge, celebrate. Anytime you finish a good week of work, celebrate. You do not need permission, just pick a meaningful topic or occasion and have a fun celebration; it will make you happy.

Ms. Drescher is a popular woman at her place of business called Tangles Hair Salon. Her friends and adult kids love being around her. The word is out on Ms. Drescher: she makes everything a special event, even a haircut. It's always fun, eccentric, and memorable. Her philosophy is to make every moment the best it can be in your personal and professional environment. She states, "It's not that difficult to find ways to celebrate. You just have to want to enhance your appreciation of life." She claims it was her father, a dentist, who modeled that to the family. She said, "My father was always the life of the party, especially with having five young children in the home. He was always playful, entertaining, and always creating laughter. He was a natural at making events the best for all of us to celebrate, even when times were hard." It reminds me of a saying by John Wooden, "Things turn out the best for the people who make the best of the way things turn out."

How can you be a conscientious celebrator? Start with being thankful. Having a heart of appreciation brings us to higher levels of awareness for what we really do have. My friend and colleague, Dave Ellis, who is an entrepreneur, a philanthropist and author of the great book called "Falling Awake," says, "I spend too much of my time looking for ways to create better circumstances and too little time appreciating the wonderful circumstances I've already created." Look closely at your life; you will discover how much you have to be thankful for. Another way to be a conscious celebrator is find the humor in the mundane. It has a way that gets us to lighten up and to enjoy. The physiological benefits of a belly laugh leave a joyful and playful impact on our state of mind and heart. It affects our breathing and our heart rate, our circulation, and softens muscles in various parts of the body, particularly our face. We often want to be associated with people who bring laughter and humor into our lives. Humor gives us a feeling of celebrating, if just for that moment.

I have been fortunate to have a wonderful friend, Richard Russell, in my life for many years. He is constantly bringing play, laughter, and entertainment wherever he goes. Have you ever met a person who either has a song, a quote, or a thought that connects to lighten up the moment that leads to joy and laughter, that leads to a mood of celebration? Well, my good and loving friend Richard has certainly added years to my life just with who he is and how he celebrates. In knowing his difficult journey, one would wonder what he has to celebrate. He never has known his biological parents; was raised in foster care, and has experienced plenty of loss in his life. Yet Richard still embraces celebration. I recommend that everyone have a friend like that.

I believe everyone should have and look forward to a grand celebration. Whether, it's celebrating one's graduation from college or retiring after years of work. I am looking forward to one of my grand celebrations, and it is traveling to Spain to walk the El Camino de Santiago, or "the way of Saint James." Tradition asserted that the apostle James travelled to Spain on a missionary journey. For centuries many have experienced the way as a personal walking meditation. It is a chance to be challenged and distance themselves from distractions of the busy world. Some may go to reaffirm their faith, search for specific answers, inspiration or new motivation. This pilgrimage is depicted in the movie, "The Way," (2012) starring Martin Sheen and directed by his son Emilio Estevez.

I wrote my 2nd book called *Blueprint for Success* (2008) in which collectively 14 experts wrote a chapter on various professional topics. A consultant named, Shannon Wallis, (Chapter 12) wrote about her personal call to the Camino which was a beautiful, must-read, inspirational story. For me, given my Spanish heritage and my grandfather's name being Santiago and my love for adventure, the Camino is calling me. So, I must answer this call; do this journey and celebrate!

Conscientious celebrators learn to enjoy their success and share with others. They feel comfortable with, "Yeah, I did it. I'm thankful now; it's time to celebrate." Celebration can take place anywhere, and it can be with many, with few, or just alone. There are many ways to celebrate your success. The important thing is that you don't miss out on celebrating. Celebrating keeps your life interesting, fresh, and alive. It is a reminder to step back and enjoy the good that is present to all of us. Having a mindset of celebrating is not new. People and cultures have been celebrating for thousands of years. Observe the signs that call you to celebrate. Here are some suggestions:

- When you open your heart

- When you notice what is working

- When you feel whole and connected

- When you appreciate what is happening

- When you have achieved something

- When you feel love from self, others, God

- When you want to enhance your growth

- When you are moved to be grateful

- When you have reached a success plateau

Conscientious celebrators celebrate life not by the number of breaths taken but by what has taken their breath away. Life is fleeting; we do not have an unlimited supply of life left in us. We need to realize that we are like a vapor here today and possibly gone tomorrow. Adopt the spirit of celebration. Encourage your family, your friends, your associates, and your clients to celebrate. Ask yourself these questions:

What would change in my life if each day I looked for a reason to celebrate?

When was the last time I celebrated?

How can I include others in my celebrations?

If you notice carefully others want you and encourage you to celebrate. They may even want to join in. We can celebrate with music, with good food, or even with a fresh cup of an organic chai tea latte, yumm! Here is now an occasion. Right before you. Go out and find a suitable way to celebrate, because you have just completed this reading and you now know what every successful person knows. Congratulations! Go now and celebrate. Then come back and apply what you have learned for greater success. Then go celebrate again. Life is to be celebrated. Remember success is sweet to the soul.

FIELD ACTIVITIES FROM YOUR SUCCESS COACH:

Taking action will help us feast from the fruit of our labor.

1. Create a collage of cut-out pictures of people having fun, joy, and laughter from various magazines. Place on a poster board; see it daily as a reminder to celebrate.

2. Call ten people with whom you are associated and gather for a party. Call it a "Celebrate Life" party and you are invited. Have Fun.

3. Treat yourself to a latte and sweeten up your soul.

Chapter Six

SIX VIP'S for Success Seekers

Successful people know that:

1. Success is being mindful of what's next. It is building a foundation of growth that is set to last a lifetime.

2. Success happens with persistence. It is taking care of the business of your life every day.

3. Success is acquired through learning. It deepens when you have fully learned the ability to learn.

4. Success is a life of adventure and endurance. A consistent lifestyle to living healthy, peaceful, and wise.

5. Success comes to the one who gives and helps others to be successful.

6. Success is an attitude of celebration. Life is worth celebrating and it must be done and done frequently.

HOW TO CONTACT US

NEW VIBE TRAINING, LLC
Carl Casanova, M.S.
11650 SW 67th Avenue, Suite 230
Portland, Oregon 97223

T: 503.372.6101
F: 503.684.6201

Website: www.newvibetraining.com

Director / Founder / Keynote Speaker / Author
Organizational Trainer / University Professor / Executive Coach

Sign up for our FREE monthly newsletter:
Inspirational stories, up to date information about all our courses, celebrations and more! Sign up at www.newvibetraining.com or email admin@newvibetraining.com

Additional copies of *What Every Successful Person Knows!* can be ordered online through New Vibe Training's website, Amazon, and Advantage Media Group Online Store. Carl Casanova has also written *Help, I am Angry!* and teaches Anger Management courses throughout the United States. He has also co-authored *Blueprint for Success* with Stephen Covey and Ken Blanchard and both of these publications, *Help, I Am Angry!* and *Blueprint for Success* can be purchased at newvibetraining.com and Amazon.com.

New Vibe Training offers personal development, executive training, and professional coach certification courses and one-on-one coaching. Whether your intention is self-employment, advancement within an organization, or self-enrichment, our programs strengthen your skills, your confidence and abilities to prepare you for personal and professional growth and success.

The Professional Coach Certification Course including the Foundations for Coach Leadership Course is accredited through the International Coaches Federation (ICF).

Index

CPSIA information can be obtained
at www.ICGtesting.com
Printed in the USA
FFOW04n0229110414
4807FF